For My dear friend +
Neighbor Gerri —

SEASONS IN A VERMONT VINEYARD

THE SHELBURNE VINEYARD Cookbook

Contributors

The team at Shelburne Vineyard is composed of a dedicated and talented group of individuals who have a passion for excellence and a love of Vermont; it's land and community. Thank you to all the wonderful folks there who shared recipes, articles, and wine wisdom. Ken and Gail Albert, Scott Prom, Ethan Joseph, Sam Coppola, Rhiannon Johnson, Macy Mullican, Steve Chick, and the tasting room staff. Thank you also to Ashley Arcury for her input early in the project.

Important contributions to the content of this book, both in print and in kind, are listed below:

Ken Albert, Owner/Founder - *Our Story: Viticulture and Winemaking in Vermont*
Ethan Joseph, Winemaker/Vineyard Manager - *Bottling, Canopy Management, Harvest, Winter Pruning*
Gail Albert, Director of Marketing - *A Commitment to Community*
Rhiannon Johnson, Tasting-Room Manager - *Pairing Wine and Food*
Scott Prom, Partner/Winemaker

Acknowledgements

My sincere thanks go to the people who contributed in so many ways to the creation of this book. First, to David Seaver for his gorgeous photography. Many thanks to Sarah Strauss for her encyclopedic knowledge of food and cooking, recipe development, tireless recipe testing, and honest feedback. I am grateful to my dear friend, Jean Hessel, an avid and devoted cook whose contagious enthusiasm inspired me from afar.

Heartfelt thanks go to my husband, Steve, and our kids, Katie, Olivia, and Nick, who provided honest criticism as well as loving support as they ate their way through this fun project. And finally, a huge debt of gratitude goes to my parents, Alan and Helen. My mother is, above all and beyond a doubt, the very best cook. She embodies the heart that is at the center of every meal, lovingly shared with family and friends.

Photographs by David Seaver
Additional photographs
by Ben Sarle, David Schmidt, and Lisa Cassell-Arms and Ken Albert
Individual photo credits listed on page 128
Copyright © 2014

Book design and composition by Lisa Cassell-Arms

Printed in the USA
by Queen City Printers Inc.

ISBN 978-0-9908296-0-7

Seasons in a Vermont Vineyard

The
Shelburne
Vineyard
Cookbook

By Lisa Cassell-Arms

Contents

Preface

By Lisa Cassell-Arms

The seed for this cookbook was firmly planted in my head a few years back when I was entertaining some out-of-town friends. They were unfamiliar with Vermont wine, shocked, in fact, that wine grapes could be grown here at all, and that outstanding wine could indeed be made from them.

I told them about the new hybrid grape varietals that were being cultivated in Vermont with great success. I explained that Marquette, a red hybrid grape that boasts Pinot Noir parentage, could survive winter temperatures that dipped to 25 degrees below zero and still produce excellent, big, dry reds. I sang the praises of ice wine and described how certain grape varietals are allowed to hang on the vine until they freeze and are then picked and pressed while frozen to extract only the sugars, resulting in a concentrated, rich, and sweet elixir that is the best thing you've ever tasted with blue cheese.

But some people need to taste to believe. I decided to prepare a dinner that would highlight our wines, attempting to craft a menu that would bring out the best in each food and wine combination from first course to cheese course. Four courses and four wines later, we had found our favorites, our friends had become devotees and I was fermenting ideas for a cookbook in which I could share some of my own favorite wine-friendly recipes, along with some time-honored dishes from family, friends, and Shelburne Vineyard staff.

As a passionate home cook, I am sent into a flurry of cooking activity by each new Shelburne Vineyard wine release. I'm always looking for ways to use wine *in* a dish as well as finding the best wine to pair *with* a dish. I've learned that simple, rustic foods are often best and really allow the wine to shine. The recipes in this book come from varied sources, some original, some adapted, and some passed down for generations. I invite you to try them and pair them with some of the exciting northern varietal wines we and our friends at other Vermont wineries produce. Remember, the wine-pairing suggestions I've made here are simply that: suggestions. The right wine is always the wine you like to drink.

In this book I attempt to evoke not only the romance of a lush vineyard heavy with fruit, but a sense of the agricultural and work cycles that mark each season. Some of the seasonal activities of the winery are explored in brief sidebar articles by our winemaker, Ethan Joseph. Tasting-room manager Rhiannon Johnson provides some essential tips on wine and food pairing principles, co-owner Gail Albert shares her thoughts about sustainability and community identity, and owner/founder Ken Albert writes about the beginnings of the vineyard as well as Vermont viticulture at present and in the future.

Vermont is a food and wine lovers' paradise. From its verdant and fertile farmland, regional specialties are emerging. We have an abundant selection of locally raised meats, poultry, produce, and fruits available, as well as world-class artisanal cheeses, award-winning spirits, ciders, beers and, of course wine. Shelburne Vineyard is recognized as a pioneer in cold-climate winemaking, producing expertly crafted wines from Vermont and regionally-grown hybrid grapes. Along with our fellow Vermont winemakers, we seek to celebrate a new generation of outstanding wines and the affinity of food and wine produced from the same northern terroir.

Our Story

Viticulture & Winemaking in Vermont

By Ken Albert
Founder & Winemaker, Shelburne Vineyard

Grape growing and winemaking in Vermont? It's been going on for millennia in the Mediterranean and for a couple of hundred years in California and New York. In Vermont, modern wine grape history began in 1997, the year Snow Farm Winery on Grand Isle and Boyden Valley Winery in Cambridge, VT, began their operations, followed by Shelburne Vineyard in 1998. All three were inspired by Quebec. Commercial-scale grape growing had begun in Quebec a mere decade earlier, and each of these three Vermont pioneers was guided by a Quebec vigneron.

Shelburne Vineyard's beginnings were sparked by a short business trip I took to Quebec for my then employer, IBM. I had been growing grapes in my Shelburne backyard with dreams of starting a winery. On that fateful trip, I discovered numerous vineyards and wineries on Southern Quebec roads. I asked myself, "If they could do it in Quebec, why not Vermont?" Our first planting was in the spring of 1998, on a three-acre site leased from Shelburne Farms with spectacular views of Lake Champlain. Grapes take three years from planting to first fruit, and it took a bit of convincing to get Shelburne Farms to agree to a

long-term lease with this one-time city boy. We planted grapes that thrived most seasons. But in seasons after severe winters, these marginally hardy vines yielded meager fruit.

While we struggled, these same varieties were being grown successfully only couple hundred miles southwest of Vermont in the Finger Lakes region of New York. But Vermont's winter temperatures, typically just five degrees lower than the temperatures in the Finger Lakes, were just low enough to make commercial viability frustratingly marginal in the North Country.

A revolution was in the making, however, with the introduction of new cold-hardy grape varieties originating in Minnesota. These new varietals, hardy to -30°F and making good wine, encouraged more Vermonters to embark upon the grape-growing adventure. Many of these new strains of grapes originated with Elmer Swenson, a Midwestern dairy farmer and grape hybridizer. The University of Minnesota followed Swenson's lead, taking on the task of developing new cold-hardy varietals. These vines, crosses between native Midwest Vitis Riperia and European Vitus Vinifera wine grapes, demonstrated hardiness to 30 below zero-and they they held the promise of making high-quality wines! Ray Knutsen in Benson, VT, and Chris Granstrom in New Haven, VT, were among the first to experiment with this new strain of grapes and their success encouraged more Vermonters to try their hand at grape growing.

We planted our first vines of this new grape family in 2004. Other growers included Bob Livingston, founder and winemaker of East Shore Vineyard in Grand Isle, and Christina Castegren of Fresh Tracks Farm Vineyard and Winery in Berlin VT.

Today, 80% or our planting consists of Minnesota-bred hybrids. These new varietals gave us the confidence to take our venture to the next level. In 2006 we purchased a 14-acre site on Route 7 in Shelburne, planted four and a half acres of Minnesota hybrid grapes, and invested in planning our new winery/tasting-room building, which opened in February 2008. As of this writing, we have a total of 20 acres of grapes planted including our original Breeding Barn site at Shelburne Farms, another on Meach Cove, our Route 7 (McCabe's Brook) site and, most recently, a site in neighboring Charlotte.

Today there are over 30 vineyards growing grapes and making wine in Vermont. As of spring 2013, 15 are open to the public for tastings, tours and the purchase of wine. Grape growing continues to expand across Vermont with vineyards scattered mostly across hillside and lakeside locations with well-drained soils and geographic characteristics that resist late spring and early fall frost.

It will take decades to fully understand the growing habits and idiosyncrasies of this new family of grapes, but we have been thrilled with our wine-making results so far. Stylistically, the wines will grow with our learning experiences and with the maturation of the vines. We are learning how to deal with the high natural acidity of this family of grapes, even when fully ripe, and its surprisingly high natural sugar content at harvest. We are learning how to round out its flavors and to coax full mouth feel by applying the ancient technique of bâtonnage, the gentle stirring of the lees, during the wine's aging process. And we are proud to be practicing viticulture using sustainable farming strategies that are kind to the land and to our environment.

Pairing Wine & Food

Pairing food and wine has the remarkable ability to enliven the flavors of whatever you're eating or drinking. While some wines are best on their own, others seem to demand that they be paired with food. Selecting the right wine for a meal can be a daunting task, but it doesn't have to be. You may have heard the old adage, "White wine with white meat, red wine with red meat," but there are more elements to a meal than just the meat. Herbs, spices, sauces, and sides can have a big impact on how a wine will complement the food you're eating.

Here are some basic tips to make choosing the right wine a little easier.

Highly acidic foods, like fresh green salads topped with chèvre, work wonderfully with wines that also have crisp, high acid, and a light body. A Vinho Verde or Louise Swenson would pair nicely. Our Louise Swenson wine consistently has subtle tropical fruit notes, a hint of minerality from our soil, a light body, and bright acidity. Perfect with any highly acidic meal you throw at it!

Savory foods should be coupled with wines that are fruity and have low tannin. This will balance the often intense and salty flavors of some dishes-think wild mushroom ragout with Pinot Noir or Marquette. Our Marquette spends some time in oak barrels, which helps to highlight the dark red berry characteristics of this wine and enhances its smooth, mild texture. Dishes high in umami are this wine's best friend.

Spice is known for enhancing the perception of bitterness and acid in wine, so spicy foods are paired well with medium- to full-bodied wines with ripe fruit character, such as Gewürztraminer or LaCrescent. LaCrescent has a beautiful floral aroma and the flavor bursts with notes of ripe stone fruits. One of our favorite foods to pair with La Crescent is sautéed vegetables with a spicy yellow curry.

And then there is sweetness. The best tip for pairing wine with sweet dishes is that the sweetness level of the food should be matched by the sweetness of the wine. Try peach cobbler and ice wine-delicious!

More importantly: Eat and drink what you love. Chances are they will go perfectly together.

~ *Rhiannon Johnson*
Shelburne Vineyard Tasting-Room Manager

Spring

First Course

Main Course

The Grapes We Grow

Dessert Course

Cheese Course

Bottling

Feta Spread
with Garlic and Herbs

Looking for a great way to use all the fresh herbs growing in your garden? This easy appetizer is wonderful as a dip with crackers, or spread on crusty farm bread with shaved, rare roast beef and arugula.

1/2 pound Feta, crumbled
1/2 cup good mayonnaise
1 large clove garlic, smashed
1 tablespoon fresh basil, finely chopped
1 tablespoon fresh thyme, finely chopped
1 tablespoon fresh dill, finely chopped
1 tablespoon fresh oregano, finely chopped
Dash Worcester sauce
1/2 teaspoon fresh black pepper
1/2 pound cream cheese, softened

Feel free to substitute 1 teaspoon dried herbs for any of the fresh ones.

Add all ingredients to the bowl of a food processor. Blend together until well combined and smooth. Cover and chill for at least 1 hour. This will taste even better the next day.

Makes approximately 2 cups.

Wine/ **Lakeview White** or **Riesling**

Opposites attract: a semi-dry white is a good complement to this slightly salty, garlicky spread.

Jean's Red-Grape Salad

Maple Vinaigrette:
1/3 cup cider vinegar
1/2 teaspoon Dijon mustard
1 teaspoon fresh thyme (or 1/2 teaspoon dried)
1/4 cup maple syrup
Salt and pepper to taste
2/3 cup extra-virgin olive oil

8 cups mixed spring greens, washed and dried
1 cup seedless red grapes, sliced in half
1/4 cup Gorgonzola, crumbled
2 tablespoons pine nuts, toasted

To make the maple vinaigrette:
In a medium bowl, whisk together the vinegar, mustard, thyme, maple syrup, and salt and pepper to taste.
Slowly add olive oil in a thin stream, whisking continuously until emulsified.

Toast the pine nuts in a pan over medium heat for about 3 minutes, shaking pan to keep them from burning. In a large bowl, toss salad greens with the maple vinaigrette. Top with grapes, crumbled Gorgonzola, and pine nuts.

Serves 6.

Wine/ **Louise Swenson**

Our dry Louise Swenson, with its hint of citrus and minerality, provides a nice contrast to the sweetness of the grapes and the salty tang of the Gorgonzola.

Stuffed Grape Leaves

24 freshly picked young grape leaves (approximately)
or jar of preserved leaves
1/2 cup rice, uncooked
1/2 onion, finely chopped
1/4 cup fresh parsley, finely chopped
1 tablespoon fresh mint, finely chopped
2 tablespoons olive oil
1 teaspoon salt
1/2 teaspoon pepper
Juice of 1 lemon

If you're lucky enough to have access to fresh grape leaves, they are at their best in the spring when they're young, tender, and freshly plucked from the vine. You can make Stuffed Grape Leaves (Dolmathes) year-round using grape leaves preserved in a jar. They're quite good and available at most grocery stores.

Wine/ **Cayuga White** or **Riesling**

To balance the lemon and herbs in these tasty bites, try a crisp, white wine with a touch of sweetness. A dry Riesling, Cayuga, or un-oaked Chardonnay would make a refreshing match.

Photo on facing page:
Basket of freshly picked spring grape leaves at our historic Breeding Barn vineyard site.

Rinse fresh or preserved grape leaves and blanch in pot of boiling water for 3 minutes. Refresh the leaves under cold water. Lay the grape leaves flat on a board and use a pairing knife to remove the tough stem from the base of the leaf. Prepare all grape leaves in the same manner and set aside.

In a large bowl, mix the uncooked rice, onion, parsley, mint, olive oil, salt, and pepper. On a board, lay a grape leaf flat with the shiny side down. Place 1 teaspoon of the rice mixture on the center of the leaf (don't be tempted to overfill or they may burst when cooking). Fold up the bottom of the leaf to cover the filling, then fold in the sides and continue rolling up from the bottom into a small cigar. Continue this with all remaining leaves or until all the filling is used.

Arrange the stuffed grape leaves in a single or double layer in the bottom of a heavy saucepan, making sure that they cover the bottom of the pan. Carefully pour 1 cup of water and the juice of 1 lemon on top. Gently place a plate or a second pot directly on top of the stuffed leaves. This will help to keep them from bursting as they cook.

Simmer on medium-low heat for about 30 minutes, or until the rice is tender. Serve warm, cold, or room temperature.

Makes approximately 24 stuffed grape leaves.

Spring Green Soup with Gruyère Crouton

Soup:
4 cups chicken or vegetable stock
2 medium potatoes, peeled and chopped
2 tablespoons olive oil
1 tablespoon butter
1 medium yellow onion, chopped (about 1 cup)
1 large bunch of scallions, white and part of
the green, chopped (about 1 cup)
2 cloves garlic, minced
1 cup arugula, coarsely chopped
1/4 cup parsley, coarsely chopped
1 cup Cayuga White or other dry white wine
1/2 cup sour cream
Juice of 1/2 lemon
Salt and pepper to taste

Gruyère Croutons:
4 baguette slices, about 1/2 inch thick
1/2 cup Gruyère, grated

To make the soup:
In a large pot, bring stock to a boil. Add potatoes and simmer over medium heat until soft. Set aside.

Heat oil and butter in a large soup pot over medium heat. Add and onions and chopped scallions and sauté over medium-low heat until soft and wilted, about 8 minutes. Do not brown. Add garlic and sauté briefly until soft, about 1 minute. Add wine to the pot and simmer, stirring occasionally for about 1 minute. Add the potatoes and stock to the pot. Bring to a boil over high heat, then reduce the heat to medium-low and simmer until potatoes are tender, about 10 minutes more.

Add arugula and parsley to the soup and simmer for about 10 minutes.

Working in small batches, pulse mixture in a food processor until smooth. Pour the mixture back into the soup pot. Over low heat, whisk in sour cream and lemon juice. Season with salt and pepper to taste.

To make the Gruyère croutons:
Preheat the broiler. Place baguette slices on a cookie sheet, top each slice with grated Gruyère cheese and broil about 1 minute until cheese is melted and bubbling.

Serve the soup garnished with the Gruyère crouton.

Serves 4.

Wine/ **Cayuga White** or **Louise Swenson**

The arugula and parsley give this soup a light, peppery flavor that works well with dry white wines.

LynnAnn's Kielbasa Pizza

This pizza can be made in the oven, but is particularly good made on the grill.

Special equipment:
Pizza stone or large baking sheet, wooden peel (optional)

**Dough for 1 pizza crust, store-bought
or handmade (see Basics, page 123)
Sprinkling of cornmeal**

**2 tablespoons olive oil
1/2 cup red onion, cut in half then sliced thinly
1/2 pound kielbasa, sliced thinly
2 teaspoons fresh sage, chopped
Salt and pepper to taste
1 cup sharp cheddar, grated
1 cup arugula
2 roasted red peppers (from a jar is fine), sliced thinly
2 tablespoons olive oil**

Preheat oven or gas grill to 450° F.

If using a pizza stone, place the stone in the oven or grill to preheat.

In a large sauté pan, heat oil over medium high heat. Add the onion and sauté until translucent. Add the sliced kielbasa and sauté until lightly browned. Add sage and season to taste with salt and pepper.

Roll out pizza dough to about 1/4-inch thick and transfer to a baking sheet sprinkled with cornmeal. Or, if using a preheated pizza stone, roll the dough out thinly and transfer onto a peel sprinkled with cornmeal.

To assemble pizza:
Sprinkle cheese onto the dough. Toss arugula evenly over the cheese and then spread the onion/kielbasa mixture on top. Distribute red peppers on top and finish with a drizzle of olive oil.

If using a preheated pizza stone, slide the pizza from the peel onto the hot stone.

Bake or grill pizza on the stone or baking sheet for approximately 8-10 minutes, until crust is crisp and cheese melted.

Makes 1 pizza, serves 4.

Wine/ **Riesling** or **Harvest Widow's Revenge**

Kielbasa and Riesling make a great match, but for something a little different, try a fruity red with a touch of sweetness.

Duck with Rhubarb-Rosé Sauce

2 teaspoons olive oil
2 shallots, peeled and finely chopped
2 cloves garlic, peeled and finely chopped
2 tablespoons fresh ginger, finely grated
1 cup water
1 cup Whimsey Meadow Rosé or other semi-dry rosé
1/2 cup sugar
4 cups rhubarb, chopped into 1/4 inch pieces
2 tablespoons butter
Salt and fresh pepper to taste
4 boneless duck breasts with skin

Rhubarb-rosé sauce:
Heat the olive oil in a medium-size saucepan over medium heat. Add the shallots and cook until softened, about 2 minutes. Add the garlic and ginger and cook for about a minute, do not brown. Add the water, wine, and sugar and bring to a boil. Reduce the heat so that the liquid barely simmers. Add the rhubarb and simmer until the rhubarb is tender and falling apart, about 10 minutes.

Remove the rhubarb mixture from the heat and strain through a sieve, pressing the rhubarb to extract all the liquid. (Set the rhubarb solids aside to mash into potatoes to serve alongside if desired.) Pour the liquid into a saucepan, bring to a boil then turn heat down to low and simmer until reduced to 1 cup, about 20 minutes. Whisk in 1 tablespoon butter, salt, and pepper. Set aside.

To cook the duck breasts:
With a sharp knife, score the skin on the duck breasts in a diamond pattern, being careful not to pierce the meat. Season on both sides with salt and pepper.

Heat 1 tablespoon butter and oil in a heavy skillet over medium-high heat. Place duck breasts into the hot skillet, skin side down. Sear until browned, about 5 minutes. Turn the duck, reduce heat to medium and cook for another 5-7 minutes until medium rare.

Transfer duck to a cutting board, cover with foil and let rest for 10 minutes. Slice thinly and serve with rhubarb-rosé Sauce.

Serves 4.

Wine/
Whimsey Meadow Rosé

The richness of the duck fairly screams for a tart and lightly sweet rosé with a bit of acidity.

Moroccan Chicken Breasts with Couscous, Cranberries and Dates

4 tablespoons olive oil
1/2 onion, chopped (about 1/2 cup)
3 carrots, chopped (about 3/4 cup)
1 clove garlic, finely chopped
2 tablespoons Ras el Hanout
(or house-made blend, see below)
4 boneless, skinless chicken breasts

Couscous Stuffing:
1 cup couscous
1 1/4 cups hot water
1/4 cup dried dates, (chopped)
1/4 cup dried cranberries (chopped)
2 teaspoons coriander
2 teaspoons cumin
1/2 teaspoon cinnamon
2 tablespoons olive oil
1 tablespoon honey
1/3 cup sliced almonds, toasted
Salt and pepper

Preheat oven to 375° F.

Heat 2 tablespoons olive oil in a cast-iron skillet over medium-high. Add onion and carrots and sauté until onion is translucent and carrots are soft. Add garlic and 1 tablespoon of Ras el Hanout and sauté for a few minutes until fragrant. Remove all to a plate and reserve.

Rinse and dry chicken breasts and rub both sides with remaining 1 tablespoon of Ras el Hanout. Heat remaining 2 tablespoons of olive oil in the same pan over medium-high. Brown chicken on both sides then place the skillet in the preheated oven and roast for approximately 15 minutes until cooked through. Remove chicken to a cutting board and let rest for 5 minutes. Heat pan over medium heat and add 1/2 cup water to deglaze, simmer, stirring until reduced. Set pan juices aside.

To make couscous:
Place couscous in a large bowl. Bring 1 cup water to a boil and add it to the couscous, stirring with a fork until fluffy and all water is absorbed. Stir in dates, cranberries, spices, olive oil, honey, and almonds. Season to taste with salt and pepper. Set aside to cool.

Serve chicken sliced over a bed of couscous. Top with carrot and onion mixture and drizzle with pan juices.

Serves 4.

If you can't find the Ras el Hanout spice mixture, you can make your own blend. Whisk together the following:
1 teaspoon ground cumin
1 teaspoon ground ginger
1 teaspoon salt
3/4 teaspoon freshly ground black pepper
1/2 teaspoon ground cinnamon
1/2 teaspoon ground coriander
1/2 teaspoon cayenne
1/2 teaspoon ground allspice
1/4 teaspoon ground cloves

Wine/
Cabernet Franc or Cayuga White

Exotic flavors, warm spice, and a bit of sweetness make this chicken a natural match with our dry and tart Cayuga. For a delicious and unconventional pairing, try it with our Cab Franc, a dry, medium-bodied red with notes of oak and a peppery finish.

Goat Cheese Tart with Mango Habanero Jam

Tart Crust:
1 1/2 cups flour
Pinch salt
1 stick cold butter, diced
1/2 (+/-) cup cold water

Filling:
12 ounces goat cheese
1/2 cup ricotta cheese
2 egg yolks
Salt and pepper to taste
1 tablespoon extra-virgin olive oil
1 onion, halved and thinly sliced
1 tablespoon sugar
1/2 cup mango/habanero jam,
whisked with 1 teaspoon warm water
or substitute your favorite apricot jam
with 1/2 teaspoon cayenne whisked in
2 tablespoons pine nuts, toasted

Special Equipment:
8- or 9-inch tart pan with removable bottom
or 6 mini tartlet pans.

Preheat oven to 375° F.

To make the tart crust:
Place flour, salt, and butter in the bowl of a food processor and pulse until the butter is the size of peas (just a few seconds will do it). With the processor running, slowly add just enough cold water for the dough to begin to hold together. Turn dough onto sheet of plastic wrap and firmly pat into a disk. Cover the dough completely with plastic wrap and refrigerate until the filling is ready.

To make the filling:
In a mixing bowl, mix the goat cheese, ricotta, egg yolks, salt, and pepper. Set aside.

In a wide sauté pan over medium heat, drizzle 1 tablespoon olive oil. Place the sliced onions in the pan and cook, stirring frequently until onions begin to brown. Sprinkle the sugar on top and reduce the heat to the lowest setting. Slowly cook onions until they become deep brown and caramelized, stirring occasionally so they don't burn. This may take up to 20 minutes. Set onions aside.

To assemble the tart:
On a floured board or countertop, roll the pastry dough into a circle, about 1/2 inch thick. Line a tart pan with the pastry and trim the edges to fit. Be careful not to stretch the dough or it may shrink when baking. Prick the bottom of the tart shell with a fork. Pre-bake the tart shell in a 375 ° F oven for about 15 minutes, or until the bottom of the shell just begins to brown. Remove the tart from the oven. If the bottom of the crust has puffed up, gently press it down with the base of a glass or measuring cup. Spread the caramelized onions onto the bottom of the tart shell, then spread the goat-cheese mixture on top of the onions. Smooth the surface with a spatula.

Bake the tart at 375° F for about 35-40 minutes. Filling should be just set and starting to brown on the edges. Cool.

While the tart cools, toast the pine nuts in a pan over medium heat for about 3 minutes, shaking pan to keep them from burning. When the tart is completely cool, spread sweet and spicy mango/Habanero or apricot jam over the top. Sprinkle toasted pine nuts on top. Serve at room temperature.

Serve with mixed greens tossed with vinaigrette for a light main course or a filling appetizer.

Serves 6.

Wine/
LaCrescent or
Vidal Blanc Late Harvest

The rich contrast of sweet and savory (with a little heat) makes a winning combination with sweeter whites like our LaCrescent or Late Harvest Vidal Blanc.

The Grapes We Grow

A new generation of cold-hardy, disease-resistant wine grapes has revolutionized the wine-making industry in northern climates like Vermont. Hybrid grape varieties developed by Minnesota farmer Elmer Swenson, and later by the University of Minnesota, have allowed cold climate vineyards to grow a selection of grapes that withstand harsh winters and short summers, while producing excellent, full-bodied red and white wines.

Marquette

Marquette is the darling of Vermont's growing wine-making industry. It is a super cold-hardy and disease-resistant hybrid wine grape that can produce rich, medium- to full-bodied reds with complex flavors of cherry, blackberry, pepper, tobacco, and spice. With the famed Pinot Noir grape as one of its parents, Marquette can produce wines similar in style and body to European reds, with pronounced tannins, moderate acidity and a deep ruby color.

Here at the vineyard, Marquette is our signature red and our most widely grown variety. Our award-winning Marquette wine is an elegant and complex balance of fruit, acidity, and tannin, finishing with a whisper of oak. It's a red that will age gracefully in your cellar and will pair beautifully with hearty dishes of all types.

Louise Swenson

A rarity among Minnesota hybrids. Louise Swenson ripens with relatively low acidity, allowing the winemaker to make a completely dry wine using a "natural", non-interventionist wine-making approach. Named after the wife of the pioneer grape hybridizer Elmer Swenson, the wine is fresh and light-bodied, finishing on the palette with a hint of pleasing minerality.

Vidal Blanc

The ice-wine grape. Ironically, Vidal Blanc is the least hardy grape grown by Shelburne Vineyard. Yes, it produces no matter the severity of the winter, but making that happen takes some serious TLC. Ice-wine is a delicacy of northern climates, a complex and sweet dessert wine made from grapes that have been allowed to freeze on the vine. The grapes are picked and pressed while frozen to extract only the sweetest juice. Vidal Blanc is a French-American hybrid grape that is the basis for much of the world-class ice wine produced in Canada and the Niagara Peninsula, and is a popular choice for ice wine production in Vermont. With its delicate flavors of honey, apple, and wildflower, Vidal Blanc is truly a reflection of our northern terroir.

Riesling

Riesling

Riesling is one of the world's greatest and most versatile white-wine grapes. This classic European grape (Vitis Vinifera) has been cultivated in Germany; Alsace, France; and Austria for centuries and is grown in cooler regions across the United States, most notably New York State, Washington State and Oregon. We grow Riesling right here in Vermont on our Meach Cove vineyard site on the shores of Lake Champlain. In Vermont, Riesling is a tender vine and is particularly vulnerable to harsh weather conditions, which makes growing it both an adventure and a labor of love.

Riesling is a grape that is highly reflective of its terroir, the soils from which it grows. It can produce a wine that may range in style from dry to semi-dry to sweet. Typically fruity and floral, Rieslings often exhibit notes of pear, apple, and tropical fruit. Our Riesling tends to a light sweetness, balanced with a crisp acidity and an underlying minerality that makes it a very happy match with a variety of foods.

Arctic Riesling

Arctic Riesling

Arctic Riesling is a winter-hardy white grape that we grow in small quantities for blending into our late harvest dessert and ice wines. It has a unique pear flavor.

LaCrescent

LaCrescent is gorgeous jewel of a wine grape that is perfectly happy to put down roots in northern climates like ours and can survive temperatures as low as -35° F! It is one of the latest and greatest in a group of cold-hardy hybrid wine grapes developed at the University of Minnesota, and we're happy to grow it on three of our four vineyard sites.

LaCrescent is a white-wine grape that typically ripens with a high acidity and sugar content. It can produce a beautifully balanced wine with a medium body and classic notes of apricot, peach, and citrus. LaCrescent can shine as either an off-dry white table wine or a sweeter, late-harvest-style dessert wine. It's a wonderful, lightly sweet counterpoint to something spicy.

Red-Wine Chocolate Cake

Special equipment:
9-inch springform pan or 6 mini springform pans

Red-Wine Cake:
2 cups of all-purpose flour
3/4 cup unsweetened cocoa powder
1 1/4 teaspoons baking soda
1/2 teaspoon salt
2 sticks (1/2 pound) unsalted butter, room
temperature
1 3/4 cups granulated sugar
3 large eggs
1 teaspoon vanilla extract
1 1/4 cups Harvest Widow's Revenge red wine
(or other dry red)

Red-Wine Ganache:
6 ounces heavy cream
3 ounces red wine
1/2 teaspoon vanilla
10 ounces good-quality dark or bittersweet
chocolate, chopped

Wine/
Harvest Widow's Revenge

Preheat the oven to 350° F.

To make the cake:
Lightly butter the cake pan(s) and then dust them with a little cocoa powder. In a small bowl, sift together the flour, cocoa powder, baking soda, and salt.

In the large bowl of an electric mixer, cream together the butter and sugar. Beat on high until fluffy, about 5 minutes. Add one egg at a time, beating thoroughly after each egg. Add the vanilla and beat for another minute.

Beat 1/3 of the flour/cocoa mixture into the butter mixture. When fully incorporated, beat in 1/3 of the wine. Continue alternating beating in ingredients, ending with the flour mixture. Pour the batter into the pan(s).

Bake in the center rack of the oven for about 40-45 minutes or until a cake tester comes out clean.

Remove the cake(s) from the oven and let cool in the pan for 10 minutes before running a sharp knife around the edge and turning out onto a wire rack to cool.

To make the ganache:
In a heavy saucepan, heat the cream, wine, and vanilla until bubbles just start to form on the edge of the liquid. Place chopped chocolate in a large bowl and slowly pour the cream mixture over the chocolate, whisking continuously until the chocolate is melted and completely smooth. Allow the ganache to cool for at least 15 minutes before pouring onto the cake.

Place the cake(s) on a rack set over a baking sheet. Slowly pour the ganache over the top of the cake, and using an offset spatula or a spoon, swirl the ganache around so that it spills over the sides coating the entire cake. Allow the ganache to set for at least 30 minutes before slicing.

Serves 6.

Riesling Poached Pears with Ice Cream

4 ripe Bosc or Bartlett pears
4 cups Riesling or other lightly sweet white wine
1 cup sugar
1 whole cinnamon stick
1 vanilla bean, sliced in half with seeds scraped out and reserved
1 pint good vanilla ice cream

Take a small slice off the bottom of each pear to provide a stable base for keeping the pears sitting upright when served. Peel the pears leaving the stem intact. Cut pears in half and core.

In a large, non-reactive pot, combine the Riesling, sugar, cinnamon stick, and vanilla bean halves. Bring liquid to a boil over medium-high heat. Add the pear halves and reduce heat to a very low simmer. Cover and simmer, with an occasional gentle stir, for about 1 hour, or until tender but not falling apart.

With a slotted spoon, gently remove the pears and set aside to cool. Over medium heat, simmer the syrup till reduced by a third, about 30 minutes more. Remove the cinnamon stick and vanilla bean and discard. Refrigerate the syrup until ready to serve.

To serve, place two pear halves upright in a bowl. Pour syrup over pears and serve with a generous scoop of vanilla ice cream.

Serves 4.

Wine/ **Riesling**

Bea's Pogása Cookies

This family recipe comes from Ken's grandmother and is a lightly sweet version of the traditional Hungarian snack.

3 cups flour
1 teaspoon baking powder
Scant 3/4 cups sugar
1 pinch salt
2 sticks (1/2 pound) butter, cut into small bits
3 eggs, separated
3 tablespoons sour cream

Preheat oven to 400° F.

Sift flour, baking powder, salt, and sugar together and transfer to the bowl of a food processor.

Cut the butter into small chunks and add to the flour mixture. Pulse just until the butter is the size of peas, being careful not to overprocess. Transfer mixture to a large bowl. In a separate small bowl, whisk the egg yolks and sour cream together. In the large bowl, make a well in the center of the flour mixture and add the lightly beaten egg yolks and the sour cream. Gently stir to incorporate and then turn the dough out onto a board or clean countertop. Knead the dough, smearing with the heel of your hand, just until it's smooth and does not stick. Flour your hands while kneading, if necessary. Take care to not overwork the dough or it will become tough.

Divide the dough into four pieces and roll one out to about 1/4 inches thick. Score diagonal lines across the dough, about 3/4 inches apart, and then cut into rounds with a floured cookie cutter or glass (about 2 inches in diameter).

Transfer the cookies onto a cookie sheet and brush with lightly beaten egg whites. Repeat until all the dough has been used, adding scraps from the previous rolling to the next batch.

Bake for 10-12 minutes until golden and set. Remove to a rack to cool.

Makes about 4 dozen cookies.

Wine/ **Rhapsody Ice Wine**

These cookies are buttery and lightly sweet with a shorbread-like texture. An ice wine with some good acidity provides a pleasingly sharp contrast.

A Spring Cheese Plate

Shelburne Vineyard **LaCrescent**
Rich and lightly sweet, the sharp ridge of acidity in the LaCrescent cuts through the richness of the cheeses to create a nice counterpoint.

Jasper Hill Creamery **Alpha Tolman**
Reminiscent of Alpine cheeses, Alpha Tolman is a mellow and nutty cheese made from raw cow's milk.

Vermont Creamery **Bonne Bouche**
Bonne Bouche is a sensual delight for the palate and the eyes. It is an aged goat cheese with a delicate and wrinkly ash rind. Salty, rich, buttery, and deliciously funky only begin to describe it.

Jasper Hill Creamery **Harbison**
Harbison is a soft-ripened, pasturized cow's-milk cheese, deep and earthy with a slightly sweet undertone.

The &@%$#! Bottling Machine!

The bottling line and I have a special relationship. I'd say it's dysfunctional. The bottling line would say I don't pay close enough attention to it, to all the subtleties and nuances that make it great. We are perpetually on-again, off-again. As they say in Seinfeld, "It's not you, it's me," but with us, it's always, "You! You $*@% machine!" I don't want to justify my use of such language, but bottling days are stressful for a winemaker. After diligently caring for each wine, six to nine months for whites and nine to fifteen or more for reds, bottling days are the final farewell. No longer will the wine be under my watchful eye. The process of going from tank or barrel into bottle, bag, or keg is like waving good-bye to your children after you've dropped them off at college: a little joyous and a little sad. It's bittersweet.

At Shelburne Vineyard, we have an automated bottling line, comprising two machines, a bottler, and a capsule-labeler. The bottler is an eight-spout vacuum filler and vacuum corker. As the bottles enter the machine, they are purged with an inert gas to expel oxygen. They are then filled under vacuum and have a final vacuum pulled just as the bottle is corked. The bottles exit the bottler and continue on to be capsuled, which is a two-step process. First, the capsule is placed on the bottle and then it is heated just quickly enough for the capsule to shrink onto the neck. The final step is label application, where a series of rollers adheres the label to the bottle.

But, just because this process is automated, doesn't mean that people aren't required to run it. Typically, three employees station the bottling line. One person works the pump and puts the empty bottles into the machine. A second person on the other end of the line performs visual quality control and packs the bottles back into boxes. And, a third person palletizes the cases. I generally stay out of the way, roaming around keeping an eye on filters, tank level, moving pallets, and most importantly, keeping the bottling line happy.

- Ethan Joseph, Winemaker & Vineyard Manager

Bottling

Summer

First Course

Veraison and Ripening

Main Course

A Summer Wine-and-Cheese Pairing Party

Dessert Course

Cheese Course

Canopy Management

Grilled Brined Shrimp in Their Jackets

1 1/2 pounds jumbo or extra-large shrimp, deveined with shell on

Brining Liquid:
1 quart water
1/4 cup salt
1/3 cup brown sugar

Marinade:
1/4 cup olive oil
2 tablespoons Cayuga White or other dry white wine
Juice of 1/2 lemon
2 cloves garlic, finely chopped
1 tablespoon parsley, chopped
Dash red pepper flakes
1/2 lemon for squeezing

Special equipment:
6-8 wooden skewers, soaked for 10 minutes in water prior to using

To brine the shrimp:
Stir together water, salt, and brown sugar until dissolved. Add the shrimp and refrigerate for up to 3 hours. Drain and rinse under cold running water. Soak shrimp in bowl of cold water for a minute or two to insure that all salt is removed.

To marinate shrimp:
Whisk the oil, wine, lemon juice, garlic, parsley, and red pepper flakes in a medium bowl. Add shrimp and toss until well coated. Let stand for 30 minutes.

To grill shrimp:
Heat the grill to medium. Thread shrimp onto wooden skewers, all flat and facing the same direction and just touching one another. Grill the shrimp in their shells until just pink and barely cooked through, roughly 1 1/2

minutes per side. Be careful to remove the shrimp from the grill when they are just barely pink, as the shrimp will continue cooking after taken off the heat.

Serve hot off the grill with a drizzle of fresh lemon juice and extra napkins.

Serves 6-8 as an appetizer.

Wine/ **Cayuga White**

Serve these shrimp with a cold, crisp, and citrusy white.

Watermelon with Feta and Pickled Red Onions

Pickled Red Onions:
1 cup cider vinegar
1/4 cup sugar
Pinch ground cloves
Pinch cinnamon
1 bay leaf
1 teaspoon black pepper
1 large red onion, cut in half then thinly sliced

Watermelon Salad:
6 cups watermelon, cut into bite sized pieces
1 pound feta, crumbled
1/4 cup pickled red onions
Basil to taste, thinly sliced
Mint to taste, thinly sliced
3 tablespoons olive oil
1 1/2 tablespoons fresh lemon juice
Black pepper to taste

Wine/
Whimsey Meadow Rosé

On a hot day, pair this juicy and refreshing salad with a bright, thirst-quenching rosé.

To make pickled red onions:
In a medium saucepan over medium-high heat, heat vinegar, sugar, cloves, cinnamon, bay leaf, and pepper until boiling. Add the onions, reduce heat to low and simmer for about 2 minutes. Remove from heat and let onions cool completely in pickling liquid. Refrigerate the onions in their liquid until ready to use.

To assemble the salad:
In a large bowl, place the cubed watermelon, crumbled feta, pickled onions, basil, and mint. Toss very gently with olive oil and lemon and season with black pepper.

Serves 6.

Sweet Corn Soup

This is a simple soup that makes the most of sweet, summer corn, fresh from your neighborhood farm stand.

4 ears fresh, sweet corn
6 tablespoons butter
1 cup onion, chopped
1/2 small red Jalapeno pepper or other small red pepper, finely chopped
1 clove garlic, finely chopped
5 cups water
1/4 cup half-and-half or heavy cream
Salt and pepper to taste
Basil to garnish (optional)
Smoked sea salt to garnish (optional)

Wine/ **Lakeview White** or **Louise Swenson**

Pair this light and creamy summer soup with a dry or slightly fruity white.

Shuck corn and remove all corn silk. Hold the corn cob in a big bowl, fat end down. Using a sharp knife, slice the kernels from the cob into the bowl. Using the dull side of the knife, scrape the liquid from the cob into the bowl of corn. Reserve the cobs.

In a soup pot, melt the butter over medium-high heat. Add the onion and sauté until soft and translucent. Add the corn kernels, red pepper, and chopped garlic and sauté until soft, about 5 minutes. Add 5 cups of water to the pot, add the reserved corn cobs (they can be broken in half if they don't fit in the pot). Bring the soup to a boil, then reduce the heat to medium low and simmer for approximately 30 minutes until the corn kernels are soft and liquid is slightly reduced. Remove the soup from the heat and discard cobs.

Purée the soup with an immersion blender, or in small batches in a food processor until almost smooth. Pour the soup back into the soup pot and heat over low. Add half-and-half and stir until heated through. Season to taste with salt and pepper.

If desired, finish with a pinch of smoked sea salt and basil to garnish.

Serves 6.

Salad with Pears, Figs, and Goat Cheese

Vinaigrette:
1/2 cup plus 1 tablespoon extra-virgin olive oil
1/4 cup white-wine vinegar
1 tablespoon Dijon mustard
1 tablespoon orange juice
1 teaspoon honey
1 clove garlic, smashed
Salt and pepper to taste

1 egg
1/2 cup Panko breadcrumbs
8 ounces goat cheese
1 tablespoon olive oil

6 cups fresh greens, washed and dried
3 shallots, thinly sliced
2 ripe pears, cored and sliced into thin wedges
(Bosc, Comice, or Anjou are good choices)
8-10 fresh, ripe figs, halved (chopped Medjool
dates can be substituted)

Wine/ **Vermont Riesling**

Pears, goat cheese and Riesling make a winning
combination.

To make the vinaigrette:
In a small jar, combine the olive oil, vinegar, mustard, orange
juice, honey, and garlic clove. Shake well. Add salt and
pepper to taste. Discard garlic clove before using.

To prepare the salad:
Lightly beat the egg in a small bowl. Place the breadcrumbs
on small plate. Slice goat cheese into 1/2-inch rounds, dip the
rounds in the egg wash and then roll them in the breadcrumbs
to coat completely.

Drizzle a sauté pan with 1 tablespoon olive oil and heat to
medium. Fry the cheese rounds until golden brown on one
side, then turn carefully with a spatula to brown the other
side, about 1 minute each side. Remove to a platter until the
salad is ready to assemble.

Arrange the greens on a platter and scatter sliced shallots on
top. Arrange sliced pears, goat cheese rounds, and figs on top
of the salad and drizzle with vinaigrette. Season to taste with
salt and pepper.

Note: If you can't find fresh figs, Medjool dates can be used
instead. Roughly chop and sprinkle atop the salad.

Serves 6.

Enjoying a glass of wine on the
tasting-room patio

Veraison
and Ripening

Here Comes the Sun

Summer in the vineyard is all about ripening. Unlike the long, hot growing season that California grapes enjoy, our Vermont grapes must bud, ripen and mature within our glorious, but all-too-brief summer. The Vermont growing season is relatively short and intense and the northern hybrid grape varieties we grow are designed to make the most of their "hang time." From bud break in early April, to first harvest in late September, these amazing grape varieties will blossom, ripen, and mature to develop the proper levels of sugar and acid that are so important in ultimately achieving a balanced wine.

In early summer, grape clusters begin to form. These young grapes are hard and green with virtually no sugar. By mid-summer, through a process called veraison, the grapes slowly but surely begin to ripen and plump up. Veraison marks the onset of the ripening process, when hard, green grapes begin to soften and change color. As they ripen, skins become thinner and take on color, and sugars develop and concentrate. We always feel a little jolt of excitement to see the first flush of color on our young grapes.

In mid- to late summer, we hope for warm, dry days with plenty of sunshine, a crucial factor for developing adequate sugar content (percentage Brix) in grapes. Pruning and careful canopy management helps control foliage growth so that the growing grape clusters have plenty of sun and air flow. As the sun acts on the foliage, ripening messages are sent to the grapes, allowing them to develop their sugars over the next several weeks. Around harvest time, we test for ripeness by picking a small cross section of grapes from different areas in the vineyard to evaluate sugar levels and acidity.

Duck Confit Tacos

2 cups red or white cabbage, sliced or shredded into thin strips
1/4 cup cider vinegar
3 tablespoons brown sugar
4 duck confit legs
1 tart apple, peeled, cored and cut into 1/8- inch matchstick slices (Granny Smith or McIntosh)
3 tablespoons apple cider
Salt and pepper to taste
8 soft taco shells, flour or corn

Optional Garnish:
1/4 cup red onion, finely chopped
1/4 cup sour cream
1 tablespoon apple cider

In a small, non-reactive bowl, toss shredded cabbage with 1/4 cup cider vinegar and 2 tablespoons brown sugar. Let sit for about 1/2 hour, then drain. Meanwhile, in a large cast-iron pan over low heat, warm duck confit legs. Shred all meat and fat from duck confit legs and reserve. In the same pan, add the shredded cabbage (drained from vinegar), sliced apple, and 1 tablespoon brown sugar and toss over medium-low heat. Sauté until cabbage begins to wilt. Add 3 tablespoons apple cider and reduce for about a minute. Add reserved duck confit meat and stir gently until warmed through. Season with salt and pepper to taste.

In a separate skillet, toast the taco shells over medium-high heat until slightly brown and bubbled. Divide the duck mixture evenly between the taco shells. For an optional garnish, whisk 1 tablespoon apple cider into the sour cream and drizzle on top of each taco, top with red onion.

Makes 8 tacos.

Wine/ Riesling

A crisp and slightly sweet Riesling makes a perfect foil for the richness of the duck and the sweet-and-sour bite of the cabbage.

Spiced Lamb Sliders with Tzatziki

Tzatziki:
1 cucumber, peeled with seeds scraped out
2 cups Greek yogurt
Juice of 1 lemon
2 tablespoons olive oil
1 large clove garlic, pressed
1 tablespoon fresh oregano (or 1 teaspoon dried)
1 teaspoon fresh dill (or 1/2 teaspoon dried)
1 teaspoon fresh mint (or 1/2 teaspoon dried)
Salt and pepper to taste

Sliders:
2 pounds ground lamb
2 egg yolks
1/3 cup dried breadcrumbs
1 cup feta, crumbled
2 garlic cloves, pressed
1 tablespoon dried oregano
1 teaspoon ground cumin
2 teaspoons dried mint
Salt and pepper to taste
6 tablespoons olive oil
Pita bread
Tomatoes to garnish

To make the tzatziki:
Finely grate the seeded cucumber into a sieve and let drain for about 10 minutes. Press the cucumber into the sieve to squeeze out as much liquid as possible. In a medium bowl, whisk together the yogurt, lemon juice, olive oil, garlic, and herbs. Add the cucumber to the yogurt mixture and whisk well. Season to taste with salt and pepper. Refrigerate for a few hours or overnight.

To make the sliders:
In a large bowl, mix ground lamb, egg yolks, breadcrumbs, crumbled feta, garlic, oregano, cumin, and mint. Form lamb mixture into 2- inch, slightly flattened meatballs. Set aside.

In a large sauté pan, heat 3 tablespoons olive oil over medium-high heat. Add the meatballs (sliders) to the pan and brown, turning as needed so all sides are browned and the inside is no longer pink. Do not crowd the sliders in the pan; they may need to be browned in batches, adding a bit more olive oil with each batch. Reserve the sliders on a paper-towel-lined plate while browning the remaining batches.

Serve sliders on pita bread with chopped tomatoes, crumbled feta, and tzatziki. Makes 24 sliders.

Wine/ **Cabernet Franc** or **Harvest Widow's Revenge**

Summer Braised Green Beans and Potatoes

The key to this dish is slow braising. The green beans should be meltingly soft and succulent.

3 tablespoons olive oil
1 large onion, cut in half and sliced
1 clove garlic, finely chopped
1 pound fresh green beans, washed and trimmed
28- ounce can of whole peeled tomatoes,
chopped with their juice
1 tablespoon fresh oregano, chopped
(or 1 teaspoon dried)
1 tablespoon fresh basil, chopped
(or 1 teaspoon dried)
1 teaspoon fresh mint, chopped
(or 1/2 teaspoon dried)
Salt and pepper to taste
2 large potatoes, peeled and quartered
Dash red pepper flakes
2 tablespoons feta, crumbled
Fresh basil, sliced to garnish

In a large sauté pan, heat olive oil over medium-high heat. Add onions and sauté until soft and translucent. Add garlic, sauté for one minute, being careful not to brown. Add whole green beans, tomatoes, and herbs. Reduce heat to low and cover. Braise for approximately 30 minutes, stirring occasionally until green beans soften. Season with salt and pepper to taste.

Add the potatoes and continue to braise for an additional 15 to 20 minutes, or until potatoes are soft, but not falling apart. Add red pepper flakes and adjust salt and pepper to taste. Garnish with crumbled feta and sliced basil. Serve warm or at room temperature.

Serves 4 as a main course or 8 as a side dish.

Wine/
Harvest Widow's Revenge

The silky richness of the dish is spiked with salty feta and pairs beautifully with a rich and fruity red.

Clambake in a Pot

This is good and messy-have lots of extra napkins on hand.

1/2 pound of bacon, cut into 1-inch pieces
1 pound chorizo, sliced into 1/2-inch rounds
1 large onion, medium dice
2 leeks, cleaned and chopped into 1/2" pieces
3 cloves garlic, minced
1 cup carrot, medium dice
1 cup celery, medium dice
3 sprigs fresh thyme (or 1 teaspoon dried)
1 bay leaf
2 cups dry, white wine
Water as needed
1 pound new potatoes, scrubbed (or other waxy potatoes), cut into quarters
4 ears of corn, shucked with silk removed, sliced into 2-inch rounds
1 pound mussels, scrubbed and debearded
1 pound clams, scrubbed
1 pound shrimp, shells and veins removed
Salt and pepper to taste
Crusty bread

In a large pot over medium heat, sauté the bacon and chorizo until the bacon is nearly crisp and most of the fat has been rendered out. Add the onions, leeks, garlic, carrots, and celery and sauté until the onions are almost translucent.

Pour 1 cup of the wine into the pot and deglaze, scraping any browned bits off the bottom. Spread the vegetables around the bottom of the pot evenly to make a bed for the rest of the ingredients. Lay the thyme sprigs and bay leaf on top. Add the potatoes and remaining wine to the pot, along with enough water to cover the potatoes. Cover the pot and bring to a boil over medium-high heat; cook at a boil for 5 minutes. Add salt and pepper to taste.

Add the corn, clams, and mussels and cover the pot. Reduce heat to medium, but maintain the boil. Cook, shaking the pot occasionally, for 15 minutes. Once most of the shellfish have opened, add the shrimp on top, cover and cook for another 5 minutes, until the shrimp are cooked through. Discard any clams or mussels that have not opened.

Using a slotted spoon, distribute ingredients over 6 dishes, ladling the broth on top. Try to avoid any grit that may have accumulated in the bottom of the pot. Serve with crusty bread for sopping up the broth.

Serves 6.

Wine/ **Cayuga White** or **Louise Swenson**

A dry, white wine served very cold is a delightful and refreshing pairing with a briny, seafood stew.

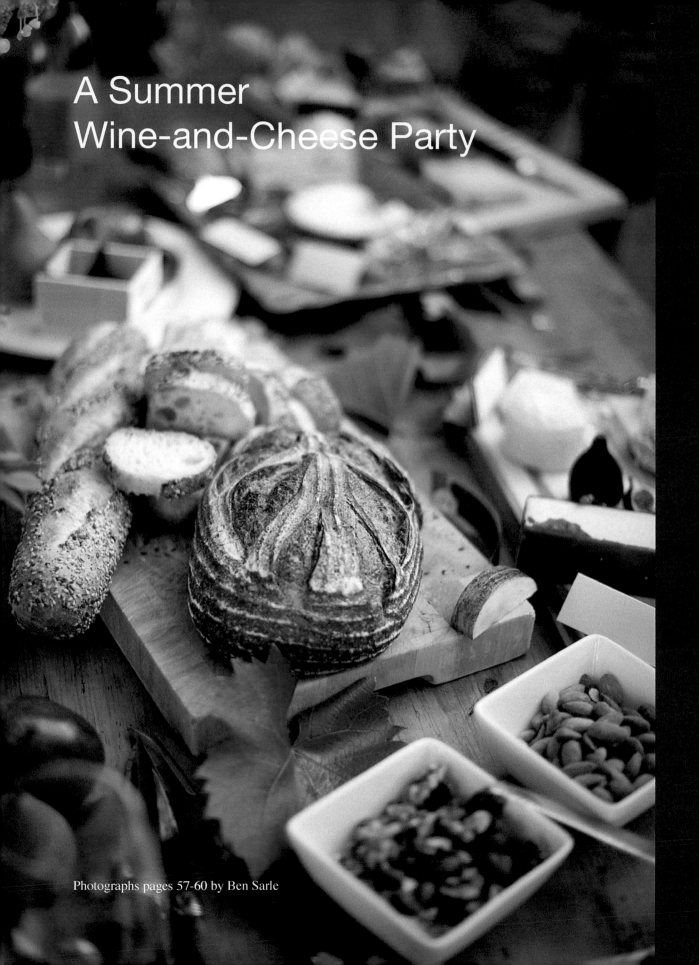

A Summer
Wine-and-Cheese Party

Photographs pages 57-60 by Ben Sarle

Bayley Hazen
Blue

Say Cheese

Wine and cheese are a congenial pairing and have been enjoyed together, across cultures, for thousands of years. Wine has a natural affinity for cheese, and when the pairing really works, it can be a fine marriage, each bringing out the best in the other. Frequently, that means "opposites attract," and it's that pairing of contrasting combinations that is so interesting and often unexpectedly delicious. Consider a rich, creamy Vermont Camembert paired with a tart, crisp white wine like our Cayuga. Or a deep, salty blue cheese combined with a rich and intensely sweet ice wine like SV Vidal Blanc.

Vermont is fast becoming known for its award-winning, world-class artisan cheeses. Like wine, cheese is a taste of place and a true reflection of its terroir, the land from which it comes. We often say "If they grow together, they go together," and with so many Vermont cheeses and Vermont wines to experience, finding pleasing combinations is a fairly easy thing to do.

Our selections for the Cheese Course pages of this book were made after much hard work, involving grueling hours of tasting varied cheese and wine combinations and then analyzing our favorites. A tough job, but somebody had to do it. And it seemed like a good excuse for a party. The cheese and wine pairings we've offered are simply our suggestions; the perfect pairing will always be what you like best together. Have fun finding your favorites.

Blueberry Ginger Crisp

Filling:
5 cups blueberries, rinsed
1/2 cup sugar
1 tablespoon cornstarch
Zest of 1/2 lemon
Juice of 1/2 lemon
1 tablespoon butter, softened

Topping:
1/3 cup brown sugar, packed
1/3 cup flour
1/3 cup quick-cook oats
1/3 cup graham crackers, finely crushed
1 teaspoon cinnamon
1 teaspoon ground ginger
3/4 stick butter, softened
2 tablespoons crystallized ginger, chopped

Preheat oven to 375° F.

To prepare filling:
In a large bowl, combine blueberries, sugar, cornstarch, lemon zest, and juice and toss gently. Pour filling into a buttered baking dish or pie plate.

To prepare topping:
In a large bowl, combine brown sugar, flour, oats, graham cracker crumbs, cinnamon, and ginger. Add softened butter and mix with your hands until the butter is worked in and the topping is crumbly. Fold in the crystallized ginger.

Cover the berries with the topping mixture, leaving a small margin of blueberry filling showing around the edge.

Bake uncovered at 375° F for approximately 30 minutes, or until the topping begins to brown and the berries are bubbling. Allow to cool slightly before serving.

Top with vanilla ice cream.

Serves 6-8.

Wine/
Vidal Blanc Late Harvest or Harvest Widow's Revenge

This crisp has a warm spice that will pair beautifully with a late-harvest dessert wine, an ice wine, our a slightly sweet red.

Photo on facing page:
Blueberry look-alikes? This is actually a beautiful bunch of Marquette grapes growing on our Shelburne Road vineyard site.

Duet of Summer Strawberries

This is as simple and refreshing as it gets.

1 pint fresh strawberries, washed and sliced
1 tablespoon sugar
1/3 cup Duet Ice Wine
2 fresh basil leaves, thinly sliced

In a bowl, gently toss the strawberries with the sugar. Let sit for 5 minutes. Divide strawberries into wineglasses and add Duet Ice Wine. Top with basil, and serve with a tall spoon.

Serves 4.

Wine/ **Duet Ice Wine**

The sweet, sharpness of the ice wine amps up the flavor of the strawberries, creating a fresh, light, and tart dessert.

Raspberry, Rhubarb, and Almond Galette

Crust:
1/2 cup almonds, sliced
2 cups flour
1 tablespoon sugar
1 teaspoon salt
2 sticks butter, chopped into small pieces
1/4-1/3 cup ice cold water

Filling:
3 cups rhubarb, chopped into 1-inch pieces
2 cups raspberries
1 1/4 cups sugar
1/3 cup flour
2 tablespoons butter
1 egg, lightly beaten

Special equipment:
Parchment-lined baking sheets

To make the crust:
In a small pan over medium heat, toast the almonds until they are golden and fragrant. Remove from heat. Reserve 1/4 cup of almonds and put the remaining 1/4 cup of almonds into the bowl of food processor. Pulse a few times until the almonds are coarsely ground. Add the flour, sugar, and salt and continue to pulse until finely ground.

Add butter to the flour and pulse until it resembles coarse meal. With the processor running, slowly add cold water until the dough just starts to hold together. Turn the dough onto a clean board or counter and press together into a disk. Cover in plastic wrap and refrigerate for at least 30 minutes.

Preheat oven to 400° F.

To make filling:
In a large bowl, toss rhubarb, raspberries, sugar, and flour. Let sit for about 5 minutes.

To assemble galette:
Turn the chilled dough out onto a floured board or countertop. Divide the dough into 6 equal pieces and shape into disks. Using a floured rolling pin, roll out one disk to about 1/2-inch thick and place it on a parchment lined baking sheet. Scoop a scant 1 cup of filling and spread it onto the disk, leaving about a 1-inch margin around the edges. Fold the edges over, pleating gently and leaving an opening in the middle.

Repeat with remaining dough and filling until all 6 galettes are filled and pleated. Dot galettes with butter. Brush the crust of each galette with egg wash.

Bake galettes at 400° F for 30 minutes, then reduce heat to 375 degrees and bake for another 10 minutes until crust is golden and filling is bubbling. Remove from oven and sprinkle galettes with reserved toasted almonds.

Cool galettes on a rack. Serve with vanilla or almond ice cream.

Makes 6 galettes.

Wine/
Whimsey Meadow Rosé

Match this sweet, tart dessert with a sweet, tart rosé, like Whimsey Meadow.

A Summer Cheese Plate

Shelburne Vineyard **Whimsey Meadow Rosé**
Whimsey Meadow Rosé is a juicy and refreshing off-dry wine with an aroma of ripe berries, fresh fruit on the palate, and a thirst-quenching acidity. Each vintage of this rosé is a unique blend of the Vermont hybrid grape varieties, Marquette, Frontenac, Frontenac Gris, and Louise Swenson.

Blue Ledge Farm **Herbed Chèvre**
This fresh, herb-covered goat cheese is light and fluffy with a mild tang and the freshness of herbs.

Shelburne Farms **Two-Year-Old Cheddar**
Sharp and nutty, this powerful cheddar is aged for two years.

Green Mountain Blue Cheese **Gore-Dawn-Zola**
Similar in style to Gorgonzola, this blue is made from raw cow's milk on the Boucher Family Farm. It's creamy and slightly sweet, with a hint of salt.

Canopy
Management

Why do Grapes Need a Canopy?

Most winegrowers would cringe at the thought of having their vineyards compared to a jungle, and rightly so. Could you imagine reaching into a canopy that may be hiding a Bengal tiger or a Brazilian wandering spider? I think I'd find a new career. Fortunately, for the vintners of the world, this analogy refers less to the deadly biology associated with jungles and much more to sunlight penetration.

In a jungle, layers and layers of vegetation overlap to prevent over 95 percent of sunlight from reaching the ground. A similar effect can be observed in poorly managed vineyards. Vines are wild in nature. If left to their own devices, they will grow and grow, creating a massively dense canopy that prevents sunlight from reaching the grape clusters on the inside. This type of growth also creates a microclimate around the fruiting zone, with high humidity and little air movement. As a result, fruit quality is adversely affected due to increased disease pressure and inadequate ripening.

Vineyard managers have developed a means to combat excessive canopies, called canopy management. Canopy management involves several practices that aim to reduce or eliminate the negative effects associated with an oversize canopy.

Here at Shelburne Vineyard, we begin our canopy management in early spring, shortly after the vines break bud, with a practice called shoot thinning and suckering. All vines will have growth from buds other than those left deliberately at pruning, so it is important to remove these unwanted shoots to reduce canopy density. We simply walk along and rub off the buds we don't need.

Later in the season, shortly after fruit set, our next tactic is leaf pulling and lateral removal. This involves strategically removing leaves and laterals in the fruiting zone to let sunlight hit the clusters and increase air circulation, all while being careful not to overexpose the clusters, as this can lead to sunburn.

During this mid-season time, we also do a fair amount of shoot positioning on our vertical shoot positioned (VSP) vines and combing of our Hi-Wire vines. These practices arrange the shoots in a more orderly fashion, exposing more leaves to sunlight.

Finally, in the latter part of the season, we hedge our VSP vines. Hedging, or topping, is simply cutting shoots that have grown too tall for the trellis system or laterals that have grown out into the vineyard aisle.

- Ethan Joseph, Winemaker & Vineyard Manager

Fall

First Course

Harvest Dinner in the Vineyard

Main Course

Dessert Course

Cheese Course

Harvest

Harvest Grape Focaccia

Schiacciata con l'Uva (meaning "crushed grapes") is the Italian name for this rustic, slightly sweet harvest bread. Traditionally made in Tuscany to celebrate the grape harvest, wine grapes are pressed into the bread and baked in an outdoor oven. Since wine grapes are quite seedy, I've substituted seedless red grapes.

Special equipment:
Electric mixer, wooden peel, pizza stone or baking sheet

Focaccia:
1 cup warm water
2 tablespoons dry, active yeast
1 teaspoon sugar
1/4 cup olive oil
3 to 3 1/2 cups all-purpose flour
1 tablespoon salt
Sprinkling of cornmeal

Toppings:
4 tablespoons olive oil
1 tablespoon fresh rosemary, chopped
1 shallot, halved and sliced thinly
1 1/2 cups red grapes, halved
2 tablespoons honey
2 tablespoons sugar
2 tablespoons butter

Wine/ **Lakeview White** or **Marquette**

Try this focaccia as a savory/sweet snack paired with a light, semi-dry white wine or as a first course together with a bold, dry red.

Preheat oven to 400° F.

In the large bowl of an electric mixer, whisk together the warm water, yeast, and sugar. Set the mixture aside for about 5 minutes, until the yeast dissolves and begins to foam. Add the olive oil to the mixture. Attach a dough hook to an electric mixer and with the mixer on low, slowly add the flour and salt and mix on low for about 3 minutes, until the dough just begins to come together. If the dough is too dry, add a bit more warm water and continue mixing on medium-high for about 10 minutes, scraping down the dough hook and bowl as needed. The dough should be soft and springy.

Gather the dough into a ball and place into an oiled bowl, turning so both sides of the dough are oiled. Cover with plastic wrap and leave to rise in a warm place, about 1 to 1/12 hours, until doubled in bulk. Punch down the dough and fold it over to deflate. Gather the dough into a ball and allow it to rise in the bowl again until doubled, about 1 hour.

Sprinkle some cornmeal onto a baking sheet or preheated pizza stone. On a peel sprinkled with cornmeal, roll out dough to about 1/2-inch thick and transfer it to the pizza stone or baking sheet.

Using your fingers, press dimples into the dough. Drizzle the olive oil onto the dough and sprinkle rosemary, shallots and grapes on top. Press grapes down gently with your hands. Drizzle honey over the top of the focaccia and sprinkle with sugar. Dot with butter.

Bake for about 35 minutes until golden brown. Grapes will be juicy and melting into the focaccia. Cool and slice to serve.

Serves 6.

Chicken Cheddar Bisque
with Tarragon Thyme Biscuits

Chicken Cheddar Bisque:
8 cups homade chicken stock (see Basics, page 123), or 8 cups of high-quality chicken broth
3 tablespoons butter
1 cup onion, finely chopped
2 cloves garlic, finely chopped
3 tablespoons flour
6 cups chicken stock
2 cups kale, chopped
1 cup carrots, chopped
1 cup celery, chopped
1 tablespoon fresh thyme, chopped
1 teaspoon dried tarragon
Salt and pepper to taste
1 cup half-and-half
1 egg yolk
Dash hot pepper sauce (optional)
2 cups extra-sharp cheddar cheese, grated

To make the soup:
In a large soup pot, melt the butter over medium heat. Add the onion and sauté over medium heat until soft and translucent . Add the garlic and sauté briefly until soft. Stir in the flour and cook for a few minutes, stirring continually. Gradually whisk in all the chicken stock one ladleful at a time; continue whisking until the mixture is smooth. Add kale, carrots, celery, thyme, tarragon, and salt and pepper to taste. Cover and simmer on low for about 15 minutes until vegetables are soft. Turn off the heat.

In a small bowl, whisk the half-and-half and egg yolk together. Whisk in a ladleful of hot soup into the egg mixture, then immediately whisk the egg mixture into the pot of hot soup. (This process tempers the egg so that it won't scramble when added to the hot soup.) Turn heat to medium and stir gently until soup is thickened. Add hot sauce to taste if desired. Gently stir in cheddar cheese.

Remove chicken meat from the bone and shred. Divide chicken meat evenly between 6 soup bowls. Pour hot soup over the chicken and serve with Tarragon Thyme Biscuits.

Serves 6.

Tarragon Thyme Biscuits:
2 cups flour
1/2 teaspoon baking soda
1 tablespoon baking powder
1 teaspoon salt
1 teaspoon dried tarragon
1 teaspoon dried thyme
1 stick cold butter, chopped into small bits
1 cup buttermilk (or substitute 1 cup of whole milk with 1 tablespoon white vinegar stirred in)

Preheat oven to 400° F.

In a food processor, combine flour, baking soda, baking powder, salt, tarragon, thyme, and butter. Pulse a few times until the butter resembles coarse meal. Add the buttermilk and pulse a couple of times until just combined. The mixture should be quite wet; add a bit more milk if it is very dry.

Turn the dough onto a cookie sheet and gently pat down and shape into a rough square, about 12 x 12 inches. Handle the dough as little as possible so that the biscuits remain tender and flaky. Cut the large square into 9 equal squares, leaving the biscuits touching on their edges.

Bake until puffed and golden brown, approximately 20 minutes.

Makes 9 biscuits.

Wine/ **Cayuga White**

This is a hearty and warming soup that calls for a crisp, dry white wine.

Sweet Potato and Beet Hash Salad

This is a hearty and filling first-course salad that can easily become a main dish with the addition of a decadent poached egg on top.

Maple Vinaigrette:
1/3 cup cider vinegar
1/2 teaspoon Dijon mustard
1 teaspoon fresh thyme (or 1/2 teaspoon dried)
1/4 cup maple syrup
2/3 cup extra-virgin olive oil
Salt and pepper to taste

Sweet Potato and Beet Hash:
2 medium sweet potatoes, peeled and cut into 1- inch dice
2 medium beets, peeled and cut into 1-inch dice
2 tablespoons olive oil
Salt and pepper to taste
6 strips bacon, chopped into 1/2-inch pieces
1 onion, chopped into medium dice
1 clove garlic, chopped finely
2 tart apples, peeled, cored, and cut into 1-inch dice

4 or 6 eggs, poached (see directions below)
1 teaspoon white vinegar

4 cups baby spinach, washed and dried
2 cups fresh friseé or curly endive, washed and dried

Preheat oven to 400° F.

To make maple vinaigrette:
In a medium bowl, whisk together the vinegar, mustard, thyme, and maple syrup. Slowly add olive oil in a thin stream, whisking continuously until emulsified. Season with salt and pepper to taste.

To make the hash:
Place the chopped sweet potatoes and beets on a foil-lined baking sheet and toss with 2 tablespoon olive oil. Season with salt and pepper. Roast, stirring occasionally until soft and starting to brown, about 30 minutes. Set aside.

Place the chopped bacon into a heavy cast-iron skillet over medium-high heat and sauté until brown and crisp. Stir frequently so that the bacon does not burn. Transfer the bacon to a large plate and reserve. Leaving approximately 2 tablespoons of bacon fat in the pan, discard the remaining bacon fat.

Reduce heat to medium and sauté the onions until soft and translucent. Add the garlic and sauté till soft, about a minute. Add to the reserved bacon. Add the apples to the pan and sauté until browned and softened, about 3-4 minutes. Add to the reserved bacon and onion mixture. Reduce heat to medium-low and add 2 tablespoons olive oil to the pan. Return all reserved ingredients to the pan, including the sweet potatoes, beets, bacon, onion, garlic, and apples. Toss gently until warmed thoroughly.

Divide salad greens between 4 or 6 plates. Divide the warmed hash over the salads.

To poach eggs:
In a medium pan, bring about 3 cups of water to a boil. Reduce to a barely a simmer and add a teaspoon of white vinegar. Carefully break eggs into a small bowl and slip the eggs gently into the water, one egg at a time. Simmer gently until eggs are soft set, about 3-4 minutes.

Remove the eggs with a slotted spoon and top each hash salad with an egg. Drizzle each salad with the Maple Vinaigrette and season to taste with salt and pepper.

Serves 4 as a main course or 6 as a starter.

Wine/ **Marquette**

This hearty salad calls for a bold, hearty red.

Caesar Brussels Sprouts

Caesar Dressing:
1/3 cup olive oil
1/3 cup Parmesan cheese, finely grated
1/4 cup fresh lemon juice
1/4 cup good mayonnaise
1 small garlic clove, pressed
1 teaspoon anchovy paste (or mash two anchovies from a tin)
1/2 teaspoon pepper, freshly ground

1 pound Brussels sprouts, cleaned and halved
2 tablespoons olive oil
1 teaspoon salt
Salt and pepper to taste

Preheat oven to 425° F.

To make the Caesar dressing:
Purée olive oil, Parmesan, lemon juice, mayonnaise, garlic, anchovy paste, and pepper in a food processor until smooth. Set aside. (This makes more dressing than you will need for this recipe-there will be plenty left over for Caesar salad!)

To prepare the Brussels sprouts:
Remove outer leaves from Brussels sprouts, trim stem end and cut sprouts in half. Spread on a baking sheet and toss with olive oil and salt. Roast in the oven until brown, about 30-35 minutes, shaking the pan occasionally so that the Brussels sprouts don't stick.

Remove Brussels sprouts from the oven when browned and crispy on the outside and tender on the inside. Adjust salt and pepper to taste. Toss with Caesar dressing (about 1/2 cup) to taste. Serve warm or at room temperature.

Serves 6.

Wine/ **Riesling**

Brussels sprouts are notoriously difficult to pair with wine, but the Caesar dressing mellows the sprouts and provides a creamy counterpoint to a crisp and acidic Riesling.

A Harvest Dinner in the Vineyard

A Vineyard Dinner

Every August or September, just before the harvest season begins to heat up, the staff at Shelburne Vineyard sit down together to an al fresco feast among the vines. It's a valued moment of calm and camaraderie before the storm that is harvest season. Our staff dinner is always potluck, with a variety of dishes as unique as the personalities creating them. Wine lovers tend also to be food lovers and cooks, and we have more than our share of good cooks on our staff.

Our staff dinner begins just before sunset. Our picnic tables are lined up end to end, draped with white cloths and set with bouquets of flowers picked from home gardens; our eclectic and colorful assortment of plates, napkins and silverware are all brought from home to reduce waste. Platters of food are arranged on the tasting bar and wine is poured for arriving staff and their families just as the sun begins to sink below the grapevines.

The dinner is always a great opportunity to try some interesting wine and food pairings, and also to pull out some library wines-past vintages that have been cellared for a few years-to see how they've held up over time. There are usually surprises-some happy (a delightful five-year-old bottle of Traminette that was still fruity and delicious), and some not so happy-but it's always an education. And what a fun way to learn!

We look forward to our annual vineyard dinner as a time to come together and share good food, good wine, and good company, surrounded by grapevines heavy with ripening fruit.

Marquette Beef Stew

3 strips bacon, chopped
2 tablespoons olive oil
2 pounds beef chuck, cut into 1 1/2-inch cubes
Salt and pepper to taste
1 large onion, chopped
1 tablespoon tomato paste
2-3 cups Marquette or other dry, full-bodied red wine
2 bay leaves
1 teaspoon dried thyme
1 teaspoon dried rosemary
2 garlic cloves, crushed
1/4 cup Cognac (optional)
3 potatoes, peeled and cut into 1 1/2-inch cubes
2 carrots, peeled and roughly chopped
2 parsnips, peeled and roughly chopped
1/2 pound cremini mushrooms, cleaned and halved (or quartered if large)

In a large Dutch oven over medium-high heat, sauté the bacon until crisp. Remove and set aside in large bowl. Discard most of the bacon fat, leaving about 1 tablespoon in the pan. Add the olive oil. Season the beef with salt and pepper and then carefully add the chunks of beef to the pan, arranging in a single layer. Do not overcrowd or the beef will not brown; you may need to do this in two batches. Brown the beef, turning occasionally until all sides are well browned. Remove beef from the pan and reserve with the bacon.

Add the chopped onion and the tomato paste to the pan and sauté until onions are translucent. Add 1 cup of red wine to the pan and deglaze, scraping up all the bits from the bottom of the pan. Reduce slightly. Put beef and bacon back into the pan, add bay leaves, herbs, crushed garlic, and enough remaining wine to almost cover the meat mixture. Over medium-high heat, bring stew to a boil, then reduce heat to low and cook, partially covered and barely simmering, for about 1 1/2 hours, until meat is tender and liquid is reduced.

Add the potatoes, carrots, parsnips, and mushrooms. Add enough water to come about half way up the stew mixture. Cover partially and cook, stirring occasionally for about 1 hour. Meat and veggies should be very tender.

Serves 6.

Wine/ **Marquette**

A big, beef stew calls for a big, bold red. Marquette, with its notes of black cherries and bit of spice is a perfect match.

Rhiannon's Red-Wine Risotto with Blue Cheese

4 cups mushroom broth
2 cups water
1 pound green beans, washed, trimmed, and cut into 1/2-inch pieces
2 cups Cabernet Franc, or other dry red wine
1 tablespoon olive oil
2 shallots, finely chopped
4 cloves garlic, finely chopped
2 cups fresh shiitake mushrooms, chopped
2 teaspoons fresh thyme (or 1 teaspoon dried)
2 cups Arborio rice
Salt and pepper to taste

1 cup cherry tomatoes, chopped
1/2 cup blue cheese, crumbled
1/4 cups walnuts, toasted in a pan on the stovetop and chopped to garnish

Wine/ **Cabernet Franc**

Our Cab Franc, with its notes of oak and spice, pairs nicely with this earthy mushroom risotto.

In a medium saucepan, bring broth and water to a boil. Add green beans and blanch until bright green, about 3-4 minutes. With a slotted spoon, remove beans and set aside. Reduce heat to a simmer and add red wine.

In a large Dutch oven, heat the oil over medium heat. Add the shallots and sauté until soft and translucent. Add the garlic and sauté for 1 minute until soft; do not brown. Add mushrooms and thyme and sauté until mushrooms are soft, about 3 minutes.

Add the rice to the pot and stir until all the rice is coated with oil. Reduce heat to a bare simmer. While stirring, add a ladleful of hot broth to the rice mixture. Continue stirring until all broth/wine is absorbed. Then add another ladleful of broth, stirring constantly and repeating until all the liquid is absorbed and the rice is soft and creamy. (The rice grains should look swollen and be soft when you bite into them.) Gently stir in the reserved green beans. Season to taste with salt and pepper.

Remove the risotto from the heat and top with crumbled blue cheese, tomatoes, and toasted walnuts.

Serves 6.

French Grandmother's Chicken

Adapted from *The Best of France*, by Evie Righter

This is a tried-and-true French classic-comfort food for a wonderful Sunday supper.

4 strips bacon, diced
1 medium organic chicken, cut into 8 pieces
with skin left on
Salt and pepper to taste
3 tablespoons olive oil
1 large onion, medium dice
1/2 pound brown mushrooms, halved
3/4 cup Louise Swenson or other dry, white
wine
1 tablespoon tomato paste
2 cups chicken stock
1 tablespoon tarragon (dried is best)
1 teaspoon fresh thyme (or 1/2 teaspoon dried)
1/2 pound small potatoes, quartered

Preheat oven to 400° F.

Sauté the bacon in a large skillet over medium-high heat until crisp. Remove the bacon with a slotted spoon and reserve. Pour off all but 1 tablespoon bacon fat. Add 1 tablespoon olive oil to the skillet. Season chicken with salt and pepper and add to pan. Brown chicken on all sides, turning as needed. This may have to be done in a couple of batches. Transfer chicken to a plate and set aside.

Add the onions and mushrooms to the pan and sauté until onions are translucent and mushrooms are lightly browned. Add the wine to the pan and deglaze, stirring until liquid is reduced by one half. Add the tomato paste, tarragon, and thyme to the pan and stir. Stir in the chicken stock and add the chicken pieces back to the pan. Bring the liquid to a boil then reduce the heat to medium-low, cover and simmer for about 30 minutes, or until the juices run clear when the chicken is pierced with a fork.

While the chicken is cooking, toss the potatoes with remaining 2 tablespoons of olive oil and salt and pepper to taste. In a baking sheet, spread potatoes out in a single layer. Roast in the preheated oven till golden on one side, about 15 minutes. Using a spatula, toss the potatoes and continue to roast till tender and golden on all sides, about 10 minutes more.

Remove the potatoes to a platter. Top with chicken and mushroom stew and garnish with crispy bacon. Serve with a crisp green salad with mustard vinaigrette.

Serves 8.

Wine/ **Louise Swenson**

A dry white with a hint of minerality and acidity is a nice counterpoint to this rich, chicken stew.

Hoisin-Glazed Quail
with Zucchini Cornmeal Cakes

Hoisin Sauce:
5 tablespoons dark brown sugar
1 small clove garlic, minced
6 tablespoons water
4 tablespoons soy sauce
4 tablespoons honey
8 tablespoons rice vinegar
1 teaspoon Chinese five-spice powder
(or substitute spice blend below)
1 teaspoon toasted sesame oil
1/2 teaspoon sriracha

Zucchini Cornmeal Cakes:
1 small zucchini, about 4 cups, grated
3 green onions, white and green parts, finely
chopped
6 tablespoons flour
1 teaspoon baking powder
Salt and pepper to taste
3 eggs
1 cup water
2 cups white or yellow cornmeal
Approximately 1/4 cup peanut or other mild oil
for frying

4 semi-boneless quails

To make hoisin sauce:
Whisk all ingredients in a small saucepan and bring to
a boil over medium high heat. Reduce heat to low and
simmer, stirring until sauce thickens to the consistency
of maple syrup. About 5-7 minutes. Set aside.

To make zucchini cornmeal cakes:
In a large bowl, toss together grated zucchini, green
onions, flour, baking powder, salt, and pepper. In a
small bowl, whisk together the eggs and water. Whisk
in the cornmeal, mixing until well combined. With a
fork, stir the cornmeal mixture into the zucchini
mixture, mixing until well combined. If batter is too
dry, add a bit of water until the consistency is loose but
not soupy.

In a large non-stick frying pan over medium-high, heat
2 tablespoons oil. Ladle 1/4 cup of batter into the pan
for each cake, being careful not to crowd. The edges of
the cakes should sizzle. Cook the cakes until browned
on the bottom, about 2-3 minutes. Turn the cakes and
cook until browned on the other side, another 2-3
minutes. Remove to a plate and keep warm until ready
to serve.

Rinse and dry quails. Cut them down the center into
two pieces consisting of a breast, leg, and wing. Place 4
tablespoons of hoisin sauce in a separate bowl and dip
the quails in the hoisin sauce, coating thoroughly. In a
large frying pan, fry the quails over medium heat until
browned on one side, about 5 minutes. Turn the quails
and reduce the heat to medium and brown on the other
side until quails are cooked through, about 3 minutes
more.

Serve the quails with the zucchini cakes and drizzle
with hoisin sauce. Reserve some sauce on the side for
dipping.

To make your own five-spice blend, blend together:
1 teaspoon cinnamon, ground
1 teaspoon cloves, ground
1 teaspoon fennel seed, ground
1 teaspoon star anise, ground
1 teaspoon Szechuan or black peppercorns

Serves 4.

Wine/ **LaCrescent**

The tart sweetness of the hoisin quail pairs
harmoniously with a lightly sweet white that has a
ridge of acidity.

Sarah's Quince Cake

Quince is a lovely and aromatic fruit that has a delicate, floral flavor and turns rosy pink when poached.

**4-5 medium to large quince, poached
(this can be done in advance-see recipe below)
2 cups Riesling
2 1/2 cups water
1/2 cup sugar
1/4 cup honey
1/2 lemon
1/2 vanilla bean, split lengthwise**

**Cake:
1 3/4 cups cake flour
1/4 teaspoon cinnamon
1/4 teaspoon salt
1 1/2 cups sugar
1 stick (1/4 pound) unsalted butter
4 large eggs
1/2 cup whole milk
1 teaspoon vanilla**

Special equipment:
9-inch springform pan

To poach the quince:
Slice the quince into quarters. Quince are very hard to slice, so watch your fingers. Peel and core the quarters and then slice into thin slivers. Place in a non-reactive pot with the wine, water, sugar, honey, half lemon, and half vanilla bean. Bring to a boil and then reduce the heat to a bare simmer. Poach for 45 minutes or until the fruit is soft and turns rosy in color. Allow to cool to a comfortable temperature for handling and then remove the fruit with a slotted spoon. For a delicious syrup, allow the liquid to simmer longer until it has reduced in volume by half and reserve for another use.

Preheat oven to 350° F.

To make the cake:
Grease and flour a 9-inch springform pan and line the bottom with parchment. When the quince are cool enough to handle, arrange them in the bottom of the cake pan in a pretty design (remember, this layer will become the top of the cake).

Sift together the cake flour, cinnamon, and salt into a medium bowl and set aside. In the bowl of an electric mixer, cream together the sugar and the butter, beating until light and fluffy. Add one egg at a time, beating after each addition.

Combine the milk and the vanilla in a small pitcher and set aside. With the mixer on low, slowly add some of the flour mixture to the butter mixture, alternating with the milk mixture until just combined.

Pour the cake batter into the prepared pan and bake for 1 hour and 10 minutes or until a cake tester comes out clean. Cool in the pan for 20 minutes. Run a knife around the rim of the pan to loosen before turning out onto a rack to cool completely.

Serves 10-12.

Wine/ **Vidal Blanc** or **Whimsey Meadow Rosé**

This delicate cake calls for a rich and intense ice wine. Or, for a lighter touch, try a rosé with notes of fruit.

Gail's Apple Crisp

With only a few ingredients, this simple and rustic crisp is a taste of fall in Vermont.

1 cup flour
1 cup dark brown sugar, packed
1 stick salted butter, chilled and cut into about 12 slices
1/2 teaspoon cinnamon
10 apples (Macintosh or Granny Smith) peeled, cored, and sliced into 1/2-inch slices

Special equipment:
6 x 12 inch baking dish or deep-dish pie plate

Preheat oven to 325 degrees F

To make the topping:
In a food processor, pulse flour, brown sugar, butter, and cinnamon until mixture begins to form clumps.

Loosely pile apple slices into a baking dish, leaving lots of spaces among the apples to capture some of the crisp mixture. Using your hands, crumble the topping over the top of the apples, covering completely.

Bake for about 45 minutes to 1 hour until topping is brown and bubbling and apples are soft. Apples will shrink during baking. Test with a toothpick to make sure the crumble topping is baked through.

Serve warm, alone, or with vanilla ice cream or crème fraîche.

Serves 6-8.

Wine/
Riesling or **LaCrescent**

Bread Pudding
with Maple Bourbon Custard

Bread Pudding:
1 cup milk
1 cup half-and-half
4 cups day-old brioche or French bread, cut into
1-inch cubes
2 eggs
1 cup sugar plus 1 tablespoon for sprinkling
1 teaspoon vanilla
1/2 teaspoon cinnamon
Pinch nutmeg
1/3 cup Vermont maple syrup
2 tablespoons butter

Maple Bourbon Custard:
3 egg yolks
1/4 cup sugar
1 cup heavy cream
3 tablespoons Vermont maple syrup
3 tablespoons bourbon or whiskey

Preheat oven to 375° F.

Special equipment:
9-inch square or round baking dish, or 6 ramekins.

Butter the baking dish or the 6 ramekins.

To make the bread pudding:
In a large bowl, add milk, half-and-half and the bread
cubes. Gently mix until the bread is well soaked.

In a large bowl of an electric mixer, beat eggs and 1 cup
sugar until light and fluffy, about 2 minutes. Mix in the
vanilla, cinnamon, nutmeg, and maple syrup. Pour the
egg mixture into the bread mixture and stir gently. Allow
it to sit for about 10 minutes.

Transfer the mixture to the buttered baking dish (or the
ramekins), dot the top with butter, and sprinkle with
remaining tablespoon of sugar. Bake for approximately
45 minutes, until bread pudding is browned and bubbling.

To make the custard:
In a medium bowl, whisk egg yolks and sugar until light
and fluffy. In a small saucepan, bring heavy cream to a
simmer and then remove from heat. In a thin stream,
slowly drizzle the hot cream into egg yolk mixture,
whisking constantly. Whisk the maple syrup and bourbon
into the custard. Return the custard to medium heat and
cook, stirring constantly until sauce thickens enough to
coat the back of a spoon. Remove from heat.

Serve the bread pudding warm or at room temperature
drizzled with custard.

Serves 6-8.

Wine/ **LaCrescent**

A semi-dry white with enough acidity to cut through
the richness of the custard, LaCrescent is a perfect
pairing.

A Fall Cheese Plate

Shelburne Vineyard **Marquette**
This dry, robust red has undertones of black cherries and a lingering
hint of spice and oak.

Blue Ledge Farms **Middlebury Blue**
A raw cow's milk blue that is earthy, crumbly, sweet, and salty at the same time.

Taylor **Gouda**
Like a young Dutch Gouda, this raw-milk farmstead cheese is
creamy, mellow, and slightly salty.

Vermont Creamery **Coupole**
Made from fresh, pasteurized goat's milk, this cheese has a delicate
interior with a slightly stronger-flavored rind.

Harvest

Crush Time

If you've ever waited in a long line for something you were really excited about…Busch Gardens, The Great Escape, the new X-box console…then you know how it feels to be a winemaker anticipating harvest. However, the so-called "line" winemakers wait in is an entire growing season long and the "excitement" is, to some of us, debatable. Instead of setting up camp outside Best Buy a week before Black Friday, winemakers get comfortable at their home away from home, the winery.

Each year, in the fall for the Northern Hemisphere, all the hard work of the vineyard crew is complete and the grapes are ready for harvest! Sometimes referred to as crush, harvest is the busiest, and by far the most anticipated, time of year for a winery. It all starts a couple of weeks before the first grapes are ready for harvest with a thorough cleaning of the winery, processing space (or crush pad), and processing equipment. Nothing says crush like staring face to stainless steel for hours on end with every size scrub brush imaginable on hand for even the tiniest little spaces. But it's worth it, because the greatest show on Earth is about to begin.

The excitement is palpable. We're tense, anxious, thrilled, energetic-we're ready. And we have to be, because once the Champagne toast is over and those first few clusters fall out of the bin and onto the table, it's pedal to the metal for the next several weeks as the magic of a vintage unfolds. For this, we employ, primarily, billions of yeast, arguably the real "winemakers." We become yeast caregivers, observing their progress turning juice into alcohol. We continuously monitor Brix, temperature, pH, and sensory characteristics, while making sure the yeast have the nutrition they need to complete a healthy fermentation. These parameters, along with all the other processing phases are checked or performed round the clock, so sleep is a luxury afforded only to our harvest widows.

~ *Ethan Joseph, Winemaker & Vineyard Manager*

Winter

Goat Cheese and Prosciutto Tartine

8 slices of crusty, French baguette, cut 1/2-inch thick
1 garlic clove, peeled
6-8 ounces fresh goat cheese
8 paper-thin slices of prosciutto
4-6 fresh radishes, sliced thin
Handful of watercress or arugula
Drizzle of extra-virgin olive oil
Salt and pepper to taste

Heat a cast iron or grill pan over medium-high. Toast the slices of bread, turning until golden on both sides.

Remove the bread to a board. Rub the garlic clove lightly over each slice of bread then top each slice with goat cheese, a slice of prosciutto, radish slices, and watercress or arugula. Drizzle the top with olive oil to taste and sprinkle with salt and pepper.

Serves 8.

Wine/
Louise Swenson

The saltiness of the prosciutto and sharp tang of the goat cheese and radish calls for a white wine with minerality and crisp acidity.

Ethan's Butternut and Beer Soup

1 large butternut squash, peeled, seeded, and cut into
2-inch chunks
2 tablespoons olive oil
2 large potatoes, peeled and quartered
2 large sweet potatoes, peeled and quartered
1 large onion, finely chopped
8 cups chicken stock
1 teaspoon rosemary, dried
1 teaspoon thyme, dried
1 teaspoon sage, dried
1 bay leaf
3/4 cup good, hoppy beer
1/4 cup cream
3 tablespoons Parmesan cheese, grated
1/2 cup cheddar cheese, grated
Splash balsamic vinegar
Salt and pepper to taste

Preheat oven to 400° F.

Spread the butternut squash out onto a large pan. Toss with 1 tablespoon olive oil and season with salt and pepper to taste. Roast squash until tender, browned, and easily pierced with a fork, about 30 minutes.

Bring a large pot of water to boil. Add potatoes and sweet potatoes and boil until very tender, about 20 minutes. Drain the potatoes, reserving a cup of the potato water. Over medium heat, add 1 tablespoon olive oil to the pot. Add the chopped onion, stirring until soft and translucent. Add the potatoes, sweet potatoes, squash, bay leaf, and other herbs to the pot. Add enough chicken stock to cover the potatoes by about 1 inch. Increase heat to high and bring the stock to a boil, then reduce heat to low and simmer, stirring occasionally for about 20 minutes. Turn off the heat. Fish out the bay leaf and remove.

Using an immersion blender, blend the soup until smooth. Or alternately, purée the soup in a blender and then return it to the pot. Stir in the beer. Return the pot to low heat and stir until heated through, about 5 minutes. Remove the soup from the heat and stir in the cream and cheeses and season with salt and pepper to taste.

If the soup is very thick, whisk in some of the reserved potato water to thin. Stir in a splash of balsamic vinegar and serve with seeded baguette.

Serves 6-8.

Wine/ **Lakeview White**

Smoky Sweet Potato Hummus

2 sweet potatoes, baked (or roasted in a microwave until soft) and deskinned
1 15.5-ounce can chickpeas, drained
1 whole roasted red pepper, chopped (from a jar is fine)
1 large clove garlic, smashed
1/3 cup olive oil
3 tablespoons tahini
Juice and zest from 1 lemon
1 tablespoon smoked chipotle chili powder
Salt and pepper to taste
(smoked salt if you have it)

Combine all ingredients in a food processor and pulse until smooth and fluffy. If mixture is too dry, add a tablespoon of water.

Serve with toasted pita chips, or as a dip with fresh vegetables.

Makes approximately 2 cups.

Wine/ **Cayuga White**

Salmon Cakes with Maple Mayonnaise

Maple Mayonnaise:
1 cup good mayonnaise
1/4 cup maple syrup
1 tablespoon Dijon mustard
Salt and pepper
Cayenne pepper to taste

Salmon Cakes:
2 1/2 pounds fresh salmon, skinned
4 scallions, white and green parts, finely chopped
1/2 cup celery, finely chopped
1 tablespoon capers, chopped
1/2 small jalapeño pepper, seeded and finely chopped
1 clove garlic, finely chopped
1/4 cup maple syrup
2 tablespoons Dijon mustard
1/2 cup Panko breadcrumbs
Salt and pepper
Cayenne pepper to taste
2 tablespoons olive oil

To make the maple mayonnaise:
In a medium bowl, whisk together the mayonnaise, maple syrup, Dijon mustard, salt and pepper, and cayenne pepper to taste.

To make the salmon cakes:
In the bowl of a food processor, pulse the fresh salmon a few times. The fish should be chunky, but not puréed. Transfer the salmon to a large bowl and mix in the scallions, celery, capers, jalapeño and garlic. Add the maple syrup, mustard and breadcrumbs and mix gently to fully incorporate. Season with salt and pepper and cayenne pepper to taste. Using your hands, shape the salmon mixture into about 8 patties.

In a large frying pan, heat the olive oil over medium heat. In batches, add the salmon cakes to the pan and brown, without moving them for about two minutes. Gently flip them over and brown the other side, for about 2 more minutes. Remove from heat just when the centers are just barely cooked through. Repeat with remaining cakes. Be careful not to overcook as the salmon cakes will continue to cook for a few minutes after coming off the heat. Serve with Maple Mayonnaise.

Makes 8 salmon cakes.

Wine/ **Louise Swenson**

These salmon cakes have a bit of heat, which is tamed nicely by a dry, white like Louise Swenson.

Bison and Mushroom Bolognese

This is an earthy adaptation of the classic Bolognese sauce made famous by Marcella Hazan in her 1976 book, *The Classic Italian Cookbook*.

3 tablespoons extra-virgin olive oil
3 tablespoons butter
1/2 cup onion, finely diced
1/2 cup carrot, finely diced
1/2 cup celery, finely diced
8 ounces Cremini mushrooms, sliced
Salt to taste
1 pound ground bison meat
1 cup Cayuga White, or other dry white wine
3/4 cup whole milk
3/4 teaspoon ground nutmeg
Dash cinnamon
4 cups canned Italian tomatoes, chopped, with their juice
Aged Parmesan cheese to taste

Add olive oil and butter to a deep, heavy pot and heat over medium-high heat until butter is melted. Add onion, carrot, and celery and sauté until softened and onion is translucent. Add half of the sliced mushrooms and continue to sauté until mushrooms are soft, about 6 or 7 minutes. Season with salt to taste.

Crumble the bison meat into the pot and stir gently until the meat has just lost its raw color. Add the wine and cook, stirring occasionally until the liquid has almost completely evaporated.

Reduce the heat to medium and add the milk, nutmeg, and cinnamon and cook, stirring occasionally until the milk has evaporated. Add the canned tomatoes and their juice, stir well, and bring to a simmer. Reduce heat to lowest setting and simmer uncovered for about 1 hour, stirring occasionally.

After 1 hour, add the remaining sliced mushrooms and stir. Continue simmering for another hour, stirring occasionally.

Serve over freshly made wide tagliatelle noodles or dried penne. Top with shards of aged Parmesan cheese.

Serves 6.

Wine/
Cayuga White or Marquette

For an unconventional pairing, try this dish with a dry, white wine that has a bit of acidity. You'll find it to be a wonderful and and surprising counterpoint to the deep, rich flavors in this sauce. Or, for a classic combination, serve with a bold, full-bodied, red wine like a Marquette or Merlot.

MaPo Tofu with Pork

This recipe, shared with me many years ago by a friend who had recently emigrated from China, was her family's version of the popular Szechuan dish, mapo tofu.

1 cup water
8 dried shiitake mushrooms
4 fresh shiitake mushrooms, sliced
3 tablespoons peanut oil
6 scallions, sliced (reserve 1 tablespoon for garnish)
1 pound ground pork
1/2 cup canned, peeled tomatoes, chopped
1 cup beef broth
1 teaspoon cornstarch
1 pound firm tofu, cut into 1/2-inch dice
Red chili sauce or sriracha to taste
3 tablespoons sesame oil
3 tablespoons fresh cilantro, chopped
Salt and pepper (Szechuan peppercorns have a great flavor and are worth finding)
White rice

Bring 1 cup of water to a boil, soak dried mushrooms in hot water until soft (about 15 minutes). Strain and reserve the soaking water. Chop the softened mushrooms and set aside.

In a large skillet or wok, heat 2 tablespoons peanut oil over medium-high heat. Add the scallions and the ground pork. Sauté just until the pork is no longer raw. Add the dried and fresh mushrooms and sauté until soft. Add tomatoes and sauté. Add mushroom-soaking water and the beef broth and simmer on medium, stirring occasionally, for about 5 minutes.

In a small bowl, stir together the cornstarch with few tablespoons of hot broth from the pot. Pour the cornstarch mixture into pot, stir and simmer on medium-low to thicken, about 2 minutes. Add tofu and toss gently. Season with chili sauce or sriracha, 2 tablespoons sesame oil, 2 tablespoons cilantro, and salt and pepper to taste. Stir gently and simmer until liquid is reduced, about 3-4 minutes.

Serve over white rice. Garnish with remaining cilantro, scallions and a drizzle of sesame oil.

Serves 6.

Wine/
LaCrescent or Vermont Riesling

This spicy dish calls out for a contrast in wine. Try a semi-sweet white with a bit of acidity to calm the fiery Szechuan flavors. LaCrescent, with its notes of apricot, is an excellent and unique match. Riesling is also a classic and delicious pairing with Asian food.

Riesling and Cheese Fondue

There is nothing more warming and filling on a cold winter day than a classic cheese fondue. With only a few ingredients, the cheese and wine really shine.

Special Equipment:
Fondue pot and fuel

1 pound Gruyère cheese, grated
1/4 cup flour
1 cup (more if needed) Riesling or other crisp white wine
3 tablespoons kirsch or Cognac (optional)
Pinch nutmeg
1 clove garlic, peeled
1 loaf crusty French bread, cut into 1 inch cubes
2 crisp, green apples, peeled, cored, and thickly sliced (optional)

In a large bowl, toss the grated cheese together with the flour until well coated.

Heat 1 cup of wine in a heavy bottom pot over medium heat. When the edges of the wine just start to bubble, slowly sprinkle in small handfuls of the cheese, stirring constantly until all the cheese is melted and smooth.

Stir in kirsch or Cognac and nutmeg. Keep cheese warm over the lowest heat.

Rub the inside of the fondue pot with the garlic clove. Pour the warm cheese mixture into the fondue pot and light the warming fuel. Serve with crusty bread and crisp green apple slices if desired.

Serves 6.

Wine/
Vermont Riesling

Riesling is a classic choice for a fondue made with Gruyère cheese. Any white with a hint of sweetness and a sparkle of acidity would work well.

Eleni's Moussaka

Meat Sauce:
1 tablespoon olive oil
1 tablespoon butter
1 cup onion, finely chopped
2 cloves garlic, finely chopped
1 1/2 pounds ground chuck
1 28-ounce can whole, peeled tomatoes with juice, chopped
1 8-ounce can tomato purée
Salt and pepper to taste
1 stick cinnamon left whole
1/2 cup chopped fresh parsley
1 tablespoon fresh oregano
(or 1 teaspoon dried)
2 tablespoons dried breadcrumbs
3 medium eggplants
4 tablespoons salt
4 tablespoons olive oil

White Sauce:
3 cups milk
4 tablespoons butter
4 tablespoons flour
Salt and pepper to taste
3 eggs

1/2 cup cheddar cheese, grated
1/2 cup Parmesan cheese, grated

Special equipment:
2-quart baking dish or large gratin pan

To make the meat sauce:
In a large sauté pan, heat the olive oil and butter over medium heat. Add the onion and sauté until soft and translucent. Add the garlic and sauté until just soft. Add the beef and sauté over medium-high heat until meat just loses it's red color. Stir in chopped tomatoes, tomato purée, whole cinnamon stick, parsley, and oregano. Reduce heat to low and simmer uncovered for 1/2 hour. Fish out the cinnamon stick and discard. Stir in breadcrumbs and set meat mixture aside to cool.

To prepare the eggplant:
Wash and dry the eggplant. With a vegetable peeler, peel most of the skin off the eggplants, leaving only a few thin strips. Slice off the ends and discard. Slice eggplants into 1/2-inch rounds. Sprinkle salt all over eggplant rounds, coating well. Place the eggplant in a colander set in a large bowl, or on a rack on large baking sheet and let the liquid drain from the eggplant for about 1/2 hour. Discard the liquid and rinse the salt off all the eggplant and dry with paper towels. Toss the eggplant with 4 tablespoons olive oil and arrange on baking sheet in a single layer. Broil for approximately 5-8 minutes or until golden brown. Remove from oven and set aside.

Preheat oven to 350° F.

To make the white sauce:
In a medium saucepan, heat the milk. In a separate, medium saucepan, melt the butter over medium heat. Whisk in the flour, salt, and pepper and cook for a minute or two while whisking. Do not let the mixture get brown. Gradually whisk in the hot milk. Bring the mixture to a boil, whisking constantly until thickened and then remove from heat. In a small bowl, beat the eggs. Add a few tablespoons of the hot milk mixture to the eggs, whisking constantly. Whisk the egg mixture into the milk mixture until well incorporated. (This process tempers the sauce so that the eggs will not scramble when added to the hot milk.) Set aside.

To assemble the moussaka:
In the bottom of a 2-quart baking dish or large gratin pan, layer half of the eggplant, overlapping slightly. Sprinkle with 2 tablespoons each of grated cheddar and Parmesan. Spread meat mixture over eggplant and sprinkle with 2 more tablespoons each of the grated cheeses. Layer the remaining eggplant slices, overlapping as before.

Pour white sauce over the eggplant and spread to cover. Sprinkle remaining cheese on top. Bake 40-45 minutes, until top is golden brown and set. Cool slightly before serving.

Serves 6-8.

Wine/ **Marquette**

This is a lush dish that will pair nicely with a big, lush red.

Clementine Cake with Fromage Blanc

Special equipment:
9-inch springform pan

4 eggs
3/4 cup sugar
1/2 cup light olive oil
1/3 cup maple syrup
1/2 cup Fromage Blanc (or plain Greek yogurt)
2 3/4 cups flour
2 teaspoons baking powder
Pinch salt
Zest from 3 clementines
Juice from 3 clementines (about 3/4 cup)
1 teaspoon vanilla

Preheat oven to 350° F.

Grease and flour 9-inch springform pan.

In an electric mixer fitted with a paddle attachment, beat eggs and sugar until light and thick. On low speed, add the olive oil, maple syrup, and Fromage Blanc and beat until just combined. In a large bowl, whisk together the flour, baking powder, and salt. With the mixer on low, slowly add flour mixture to the egg mixture, occasionally scraping the sides of the bowl. Mix just until smooth, about 1 minute.

Wash and dry clementines. Using a microplane, zest the clementines and add the zest to the batter. Juice the clementines and add the juice to the batter. Add vanilla and mix until just combined.

Pour the batter into the prepared pan and bake for approximately 45 minutes or until skewer inserted into the center of the cake comes out clean.

Cool and release from pan. Serve with fresh whipped cream if desired.

Serves 8-10.

Wine/
Vidal Blanc Ice Wine or **Duet Ice Wine**

This is a rustic and not-too-sweet cake. A late-harvest or sweet ice wine provide a nice contrast.

Almond Fennel Biscotti with Ice Wine

1/2 cup sliced almonds, toasted
1/2 teaspoon fennel seeds
1 stick butter, room temperature
3/4 cup sugar
2 large eggs
1 teaspoon vanilla
1 teaspoon lemon zest
2 1/4 cups all-purpose flour
1 1/2 teaspoons baking powder
1/4 teaspoon salt
3-ounces dried Medjool dates (approximately 4 dates), chopped

Preheat oven to 350° F.

In a sauté pan over medium heat, toast almonds until lightly brown. Set aside. In the same pan, toast fennel seeds until fragrant. Add to almonds and set aside till cool, then chop to medium fine.

In an electric mixer fitted with a paddle attachment, beat the butter and sugar on medium until smooth and fluffy, about 2 minutes, scraping the bowl occasionally. Add eggs, vanilla, and zest and beat until creamy and light, about 2 more minutes.

In another bowl, whisk together the flour, baking powder and salt. Slowly add flour mixture to the butter mixture, mixing on low speed until just incorporated. Add the reserved chopped almonds, fennel seeds, and chopped dates and mix on low for 1 minute to distribute.

Remove dough onto a clean surface and divide in quarters. Form 4 logs approximately 1 1/2 inches wide by 9 inches long and place on an ungreased baking sheet. Bake until lightly browned, about 25-30 minutes.

Remove from oven and cool slightly. Lower oven temperature to 275° F. Using serrated bread knife, carefully slice the logs on a diagonal, into 1/2-inch thick slices.

Arrange biscotti on their sides on the baking sheet. Return to the oven and bake until golden and crisp, about 10 minutes. Turn the biscotti over and bake the other side for about 5-10 more minutes.

Makes approximately 3 dozen.

Wine/
Rhapsody Ice Wine

In Italy, biscotti are traditionally dipped into a glass of Vin Santo at the end of a meal. For a distinctly Vermont take, try these with a glass of ice wine, and don't forget to dip.

Harvest Widow's Bonbons

Truffles:
8 ounces good bittersweet chocolate (60% cacao), finely chopped
1/2 cup heavy cream
1/2 cup Harvest Widow's Revenge, or other fruity red wine
Peel from 1/2 orange
Pinch salt

Coating Options:
2 tablespoons unsweetened cocoa powder
1/8 cup pistachios, finely ground
1/8 cup almonds, finely ground

Place the chopped chocolate in a large, heat-proof bowl. In a small saucepan, heat the cream, wine, and orange peel until just boiling. Remove from heat and discard the orange peel. Slowly pour the hot cream and wine mixture over the chopped chocolate, whisking until all the chocolate is melted and mixture is smooth. Whisk in a pinch of salt.

Allow mixture to cool to room temperature and then refrigerate until a bit firm, about 15 minutes. Using a tablespoon, scoop balls of chocolate onto a parchment-lined baking sheet. Refrigerate the truffles until firm, about 15 minutes.

Roll the truffles in the cocoa powder, chopped pistachios, chopped almonds, or an assortment of all three and refrigerate until ready to serve.

Makes about 20 truffles.

Wine/
Harvest Widow's Revenge

Bittersweet chocolate and red wine are a voluptuous combination. Harvest Widow's Revenge is rich and fruity and makes a decadent and delicious pairing.

A Winter Cheese Plate

Shelburne Vineyard **Vidal Blanc Ice Wine**
A gorgeously rich and sweet wine made from Vidal Blanc grapes picked while frozen on the vine and pressed while frozen so that only the sugars are extracted. A decadent counterpoint to the cheeses below.

Thistle Hill Farm **Tarentaise**
Tarentaise is a unique aged hard cheese made from raw cow's milk. It has a sharp bite with a nutty and slightly salty flavor, a dense and crumbly texture, and a long finish.

Jasper Hill Farm **Bayley Hazen Blue**
Made from raw cow's milk, Bayley Hazen Blue is dense, rich, and salty with a sharp veining of blue and a nutty finish.

Blythedale **Camembert VT**
A delicious, creamy, buttery Camembert with a delicate rind.

Ice Wine

Ice wine is a sweet, complex, and gorgeously balanced dessert wine that is a specialty of cold climates like ours and a unique taste of place. The first true ice wine was made in Germany in the late 18th century. A happy accident resulting from an unexpected early freeze, these sweet, concentrated wines were a rare treat, yet they were not systematically produced until 100 years later.

Today, ice wine is produced from a variety of different grapes. At Shelburne Vineyard we use Vidal Blanc and Arctic Riesling grapes to make ours. The secret of ice wine lies in the concentration of sugar and acidity, and to achieve this, the grapes are left to hang on the vine into the winter months until they freeze. By then the foliage has fallen off leaving the grapes exposed, so the crop must be covered with netting to keep the birds away.

When the temperature reaches about 15° F, usually by mid-December, the grapes are ready to harvest. They are picked by hand, often at night or early morning to insure they remain frozen, and then pressed while they are frozen. By doing this, only the slushy sugar in the grape is extracted, leaving the frozen water behind. The result is a very small yield of concentrated, intense juice high in sugar and acidity. We ferment our ice wine in stainless tanks and then allow it to age in the bottle for a few months to achieve the full-bodied complexity that makes ice wine so alluring.

SHELBURNE VINEYARD

Rhapsody

ICE WINE

2012 VERMONT GROWN

Shave and a Haircut

Winter is a sleepy time for a vineyard. It must look cold standing out there, appendages naked and exposed, with no woodstove or goose down blanket for warmth, but winter dormancy is an important stage in the cycle of a grapevine. With the onset of fall and after the first frost, the leaves of the grapevine drop off. No longer able to produce carbohydrates from photosynthesis, the grapevine effectively winterizes itself for protection against months of cold. Here in Vermont, that period is about five months. But it isn't all rest and relaxation, at least not for us winegrowers. We're an opportunistic bunch, and take advantage of this time to give the vines the same thing grandmothers want to give their grandsons, a haircut and a shave.

The grooming I refer to is called dormant grapevine pruning. The goal of winegrape pruning is to balance the vegetative (shoots and leaves) and reproductive (grapes) growth of the vines, so that maximum crop quality and quantity can be achieved. The vine's seasonal growth, one-year-old canes, are used to determine the number of fruiting buds left on the vine to produce fruit for the coming season. Each winter, between January and March, we remove 80%-85% of the vines seasonal growth. If we simply decided to skip this step, our vineyard rows would look more like the sprawling, spideresque vines you see along roads and rivers. The task of the vineyard team is to control these miscreant tendencies of the vines and contain their growth to the designated spacing within the vineyard.

- Ethan Joseph, Winemaker & Vineyard Manager

Winter
Pruning

A Commitment to Community

By Gail Albert, Co-owner & Director of Marketing

When we founded Shelburne Vineyard in 1998, both Ken and I had come from two decades of community involvement. We'd volunteered in local political and environmental affairs and I'd been a service-learning educator working with non-profits and helping students learn through community engagement. So when we started this venture, those threads of commitment helped forge our mission. Sustainability, environmental responsibility, and community engagement became key to so many of our decisions and have doubled the satisfaction and rewards of this adventure.

Sustainability

With our shared love and respect for the environment, we grow our grapes sustainably on lands perpetually deeded to agriculture, grassing the rows to prevent erosion and using sustainable disease- and pest-control practices to minimize the use of harmful substances needed to produce a healthy crop. Our local architect, Steve Selin, used local materials whenever possible, minimized the use of resources, and helped design our building to LEED standards. In so many ways our winery reflects the local terroir-our cherrywood tasting bar from a tree harvested at Shelburne Farms, our light fixtures crafted by a local metalsmith, concrete floors infused with colorful local stone, and walls fabricated in nearby Hinesburg.

Our Vineyard Adventure

I treasure Vermont's sense of community and love to engage our neighbors in our vineyard adventure. We were fortunate to be mentored by a generous Quebec vintner and we try to recycle that knowledge! A class of Waldorf preschoolers helped plant our first crop, each planting a bare-root vine, learning about the land and how things grow. As graduating eigth graders, they returned to help harvest their bounty! Many of our early helpers were interns and volunteers from local high schools and colleges who experienced and learned here and developed their own skills and passions. One is now a prestigious Santa Barbara winemaker; another owns her own Vermont vineyard and farm; and Ethan Joseph has evolved to become our Winemaker and Vineyard Manager. And, as pioneers in Vermont viticulture and winemaking, we pass that mentoring along to newcomers on this journey of northern viticulture

.

Vermont has allowed us to fulfill our dreams, and we try to help others fulfill theirs.

Community Events

Our beautiful winery has a life of its own with free festivals and concerts featuring our colleagues in Vermont's localvore and artistic renaissance, and we offer our space for weddings, parties, and non-profit events. We've had yoga among the vines, poetry nights, and viticulture classes as other ways to bring our friends and neighbors together and each summer is punctuated by a big staff potluck. Even harvest has become a community celebration-customers and friends and community organizations, like Refugee Resettlement, help us bring in the crop, share a meal, and earn a day's pay.

Our favorite event is our pre-Thanksgiving Annual Wine Festival and Food Drive where we bring together local food producers and the Emergency Food Shelf and invite the public to come taste in exchange for donations of non-perishable foods—and we raise over 3000 pounds of food in a day! When Hurricane Irene devastated many Vermont farms and spared ours, we created a new wine, "In Spite of Irene", contributing a portion of the proceeds to the Vermont Farmers' Relief Fund to help them recover. Each of our monthly First Thursday local singer-songwriter concerts partners with a local non-profit who share their mission with the crowd receive a portion of profits of the evening's wine sales.

I'd like to think that one day, some of the local kids who come to these events with their parents will find their own passions and make their mark in this beautiful Vermont where we make our homes and that their memories of sharing our experience helped inspire their dreams!

Basics

Pizza Dough

Special Equipment:
Standing mixer with dough-hook attachment

1 cup lukewarm water
1 tablespoon sugar
1 package active dry yeast (2 1/4 teaspoons dry yeast)
2 1/4 cups flour
1 cup cake flour
1 tablespoon salt
2 tablespoons olive oil

In a large bowl of a standing mixer, combine the water, sugar, and yeast. Allow yeast to start to bubble, about 5 minutes. Stir in the flour, cake flour, and salt. Add the oil to the yeast and flour mixture and, using the dough hook, knead the mixture on low speed for about 10 minutes, until smooth and no longer sticky.

Place the dough in a lightly oiled bowl, and turn to coat both sides. Cover the dough with plastic wrap and let rise in a warm place until doubled, about 2 hours.

Punch the dough down and divide it into two balls. Cover the dough with plastic wrap or a clean dish towel and let it rise in a warm place for another hour.

Makes enough dough for 2 large pizzas or 4 small pizzas.

Chicken Stock

2 quarts water
2 large chicken breasts, bone in (skin removed)
1 large carrot, scrubbed but not peeled, and coarsely chopped
2 stalks celery, coarsely chopped
1/2 onion, coarsely chopped
1 clove garlic, smashed
1 bay leaf
1 teaspoon dried thyme
1 teaspoon dried tarragon
Salt and pepper to taste

Bring the water to boil in a large stock pot. Add all stock ingredients, return to a boil, then reduce heat to a slow simmer. Cover and simmer on the lowest heat for approximately 2 hours, skimming occasionally to remove any scum or excess fat. Strain the stock into a large pot and keep hot on the stove. Reserve the chicken breasts for another use. Discard the vegetables.

Makes about 8 cups of stock.

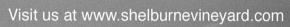
Visit us at www.shelburnevineyard.com

Recipe Contributors:

The recipes listed below were contributed by family, friends, and Shelburne Vineyard staff. All other recipes in this book were contributed by **Lisa Cassell-Arms**.

Gail Albert
Duck Confit Tacos
Apple Crisp
Bea's Pogásca Cookies

Ethan Joseph
Butternut and Beer Soup

Rhiannon Johnson
Red-Wine Risotto with Blue Cheese

LynnAnn Prom
Kielbasa Pizza

Helen Cassell
Eleni's Moussaka
Stuffed Grape Leaves

Jean Hessel
Red-Grape Salad
Grilled Brined Shrimp in Their Jackets

Sarah Strauss
Quince Cake
Red-Wine Chocolate Cake
Clambake in a Pot

Stephanie Strouse
Duet of Summer Strawberries
Smoky Sweet Potato Hummus

Photo Credits:

All photographs by **David Seaver,** with the exception of the following:

Ben Sarle: pages 57, 58, 59, 60

Lisa Cassell-Arms: pages 7, 18, 25, 26, 27 bottom, 28, 29, 30, 33, 37, 38, 39, 43, 44, 45, 47, 50, 61, 62, 71, 95, 96, 97, 99, 103, 104, 111, 112, 114, 118, 125, 126

David Schmidt: page 4

Ken Albert: pages 13, 34

Resources:

For the recipes in this book, I've made every effort to use local, regional, fresh, and seasonal foods and products wherever possible. While by no means complete, the following list includes some of the wonderful products and resources that I have used here. I encourage you to seek out local and regional favorites of your own!

Winemaking and Grape-Growing Resources
NE Vine Supply
VT Grape & Wine Council

Food Producers and Products
Artesano
Cavendish Game Birds
Fat Toad Farm
Green Mountain Goodness
Jericho Settlers Farm
King Arthur Flour
Lake Champlain Chocolates
Misty Knoll Farms
O Bread Bakery
Olivia's Croutons
Pete's Greens
Sidehill Farm Jams
Teeny Tiny Spice Co. of Vermont

Cheesemakers
Blue Ledge Farm
Blythedale Farm
Cellars at Jasper Hill
Green Mountain Blue Cheese and Boucher
Family Farm
Jasper Hill Farm
Lazy Lady Farm
Shelburne Farms
Taylor Farm
Thistle Hill Farm
Vermont Creamery

Other
Jeremy Ayers Pottery (plate seen on page 116)

Wine Pairing Index

Wine pairings. See also specific wines below
basic tips for, 11–12

Cabernet Franc
Moroccan Chicken Breasts with Couscous, Cranberries and Dates, 24
Rhiannon's Red-Wine Risotto with Blue Cheese, 84
Spiced Lamb Sliders with Tzatziki, 53

Cayuga White
Bison and Mushroom Bolognese, 103
Chicken Cheddar Bisque with Tarragon Thyme Biscuits, 75
Clambake in a Pot, 55
Grilled Brined Shrimp in their Jackets, 41
Moroccan Chicken Breasts with Couscous, Cranberries and Dates, 24
Smoky Sweet Potato Hummus, 101
Spring Green Soup with Gruyère Crouton, 19
Stuffed Grape Leaves, 18

Duet Ice Wine
Clementine Cake with Fromage Blanc, 111
Duet of Summer Strawberries, 63

Harvest Widow's Revenge
Blueberry Ginger Crisp, 61
Harvest Widow's Bonbons, 114
Kielbasa Pizza, 21
Red-Wine Chocolate Cake, 31
Spiced Lamb Sliders with Tzatziki, 53
Summer Braised Green Beans & Potatoes, 54

LaCrescent
Bread Pudding with Maple Bourbon Custard, 92
Gail's Apple Crisp, 91
Goat Cheese Tart with Mango Habanero Jam, 25
Hoisin-Glazed Quail with Zucchini Cornmeal Cakes, 87
MaPo Tofu with Pork, 106
Spring Cheese Plate, 35

Lakeview White
Ethan's Butternut and Beer Soup, 100
Feta Spread with Garlic & Herbs, 15
Harvest Grape Focaccia, 73
Sweet Corn Soup, 46

Louise Swenson
Clambake in a Pot, 55
French Grandmother's Chicken, 86
Goat Cheese and Prosciutto Tartine, 99
Jean's Red-Grape Salad, 16
Salmon Cakes with Maple Mayonnaise, 102
Spring Green Soup with Gruyère Crouton, 19
Sweet Corn Soup, 46

Marquette
Bison and Mushroom Bolognese, 103
Eleni's Moussaka, 109
Fall Cheese Plate, 93
Harvest Grape Focaccia, 73
Marquette Beef Stew, 83
Sweet Potato and Beet Hash Salad, 77

Rhapsody Ice Wine
Almond Fennel Biscotti with Ice Wine, 113
Bea's Pogása Cookies, 34

Riesling
Caesar Brussels Sprouts, 78
Duck Confit Tacos, 52
Feta Spread with Garlic & Herbs, 15
Gail's Apple Crisp, 91
LynnAnn's Kielbasa Pizza, 21
Riesling Poached Pears with Ice Cream, 33
Stuffed Grape Leaves, 18

Vermont Riesling
MaPo Tofu with Pork, 106
Riesling and Cheese Fondue, 107
Salad with Pears, Figs and Goat Cheese, 47
Vidal Blanc Ice Wine
Clementine Cake with Fromage Blanc, 111
Sarah's Quince Cake, 90
Winter Cheese Plate, 115

Vidal Blanc Late Harvest
Blueberry Ginger Crisp, 61
Goat Cheese Tart with Mango Habanero Jam, 25

Whimsey Meadow Rosé
Duck with Rhubarb-Rosé Sauce, 23
Raspberry, Rhubarb and Almond Galette, 66
Sarah's Quince Cake, 90
Summer Cheese Plate, 67
Watermelon with Feta and Pickled Red Onions, 43

General Index

Note: Page references in italics indicate recipe photographs.

harvest time, 96

history of, 9–10

ice wines, about, 117

LaCrescent grapes, 30

Louise Swenson grapes, 28

Marquette grapes, 27

Riesling grapes, 29

sustainability measures, 121

Vidal Blanc grapes, 28

Shrimp

Clambake in a Pot, 55, 56

Grilled Brined, in their Jackets, 41, 42

Sliders, Spiced Lamb, with Tzatziki, 53, 53

Smoky Sweet Potato Hummus, 101, 101

Soups. See also Stews

Butternut and Beer, Ethan's, 100, 100

Chicken Cheddar Bisque with Tarragon Thyme Biscuits, 75, 76

Spring Green, with Gruyère Crouton, 19, 20

Sweet Corn, 46

Spinach

Sweet Potato and Beet Hash Salad, 77

Squash

Ethan's Butternut and Beer Soup, 100, 100

Hoisin-Glazed Quail with Zucchini Cornmeal Cakes, 87, 88

Stews

French Grandmother's Chicken, 85, 86

Marquette Beef, 83, 83

Strawberries, Summer, Duet of, 63, 64

Stuffed Grape Leaves, 18, 18

Sweet Potato(es)

and Beet Hash Salad, 77

Ethan's Butternut and Beer Soup, 100, 100

Hummus, Smoky, 101, 101

T

Tacos, Duck Confit, 51, 52

Tarragon Thyme Biscuits, Chicken Cheddar Bisque with, 75, 76

Tartine, Goat Cheese and Prosciutto, 99, 99

Tarts

Goat Cheese, with Mango Habanero Jam, 25, 25–26

Raspberry, Rhubarb and Almond Galette, 65, 66

Thyme Tarragon Biscuits, Chicken Cheddar Bisque with, 75, 76

Tofu, MaPo, with Pork, 105, 106

Tomatoes

Bison and Mushroom Bolognese, 103, 103

Eleni's Moussaka, 109, 110

Rhiannon's Red-Wine Risotto with Blue Cheese, 84

Summer Braised Green Beans & Potatoes, 54, 54

Tzatziki, Spiced Lamb Sliders with, 53, 53

V

Vegetables. See specific vegetables

W

Watermelon with Feta and Pickled Red Onions, 43, 43

Z

Zucchini Cornmeal Cakes, Hoisin-Glazed Quail with, 87, 88